P9-DCI-754

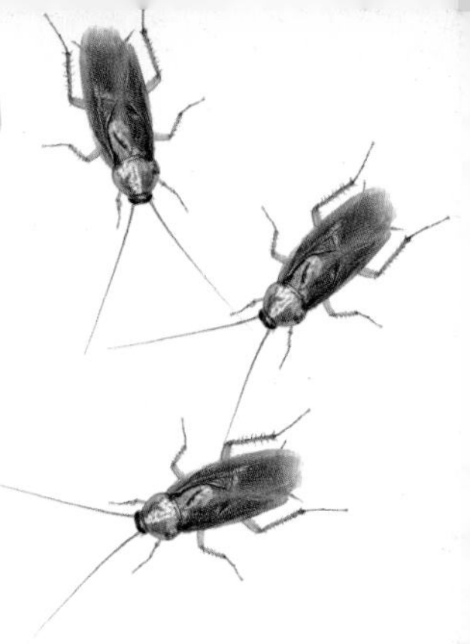

That's GROSS!

BY CRISPIN BOYER

WASHINGTON, D.C.

GROSS Contents

Meet Your Gross Host!

Meet Your Gross Host!

HI THERE! I'M DARYL. I'm a dung beetle. Like all dung beetles, I eat poop. I roll it into balls, too, and then push the balls all over the place. It's kind of my thing, but people think it's nasty. I guess that makes me the perfect host to introduce you to the world of everything gross!

Why in the world would you want to engage your gag reflex? According to the scientists who study these things, disgust is crucial to human survival. People evolved a sense of revulsion to protect them from eating icky things and sticking their fingers in stuff that could make them sick. See, a sense of grossness is good for you!

But before we get the dung ball rolling, let's make sure you know what you're in for.

This book isn't called *That's Cute* or even *That's Mildly Disconcerting.* It's *That's Gross!* If all goes according to plan, this will be the most disgustingly awesome book you've ever read!

You're about to see things that you can't unsee, such as tongue-eating sea monsters and wasps that turn cockroaches into zombies. You're going to learn things you'll never forget, including the real scoop on poop and the truth about toe jam. By the time you've put down *That's Gross!*, you'll know which insect tastes like a Jolly Rancher, what object in your pocket has more germs than a toilet seat, and why you should never—ever—squat to pee in the Amazon River. My, won't dinnertime conversation be fun at your house!

Now that you've been warned, let's get gross! Oh, and look for me on the pages where you want some nasty bonus knowledge. Until then, I gotta roll!

How to Get the Most From *That's* GROSS!

STEP 1: LIMBER UP!

QUICK: Wrinkle your nose, furrow your forehead, and stick out your tongue. Good. Now, do it again. And . . . one more time. Psychologists call this puckered expression the "gape face" or "yuck face." All people make it when they see something repulsive. It's no coincidence that the yuck face involves the same facial muscles that come into play when you puke. Practice your gape face now, and you might be less likely to upchuck later, like when you get to the part of the book about dining on a snake heart . . . while it's still beating!

STEP 2: CHECK YOUR GROSS GLOSSARY!

This book is full of fancy—and not-too-fancy—terms for foul fluids and other nasty substances. If you're ever stumped about the meaning of a word, flip back to this gross glossary for a repulsive refresher.

BARF: Puke, spew, throw up, toss cookies, upchuck, vomit

BURP: Belch

PASS GAS: Break wind, flatulence, poot, toot

GERM: Microbe

PEE: Number one, urine, wee, whiz

POOP: Bowel movement, doodie, doo-doo, dookie, dung, excrement, fecal matter, feces, number two, poo, scat, stool

SNOT: Boogers, mucus, slime

SPIT: Saliva, spittle

STEP 3: GET READY TO RATE!

It was a disgusting job, but somebody had to do it! Our horrible host, Daryl the Dung Beetle, rated this book's troubling topics in order of grossness. You'll find the results on the Gag Gauge at the end of each chapter. Don't agree with the results? Make your own Gag Gauge and poll your pals!

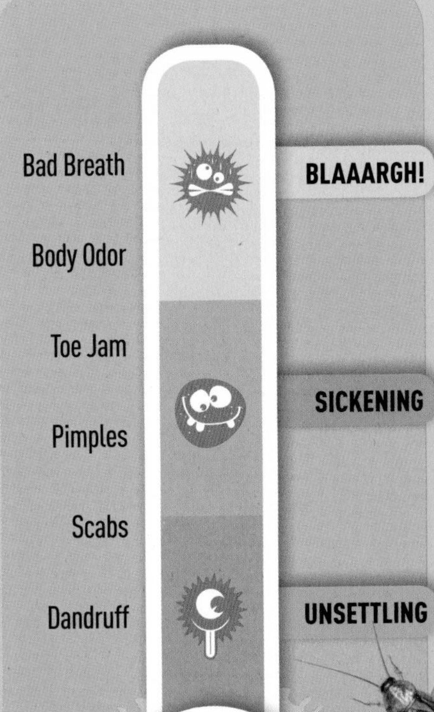

Welcome to Your HAPPY Place!

It's a Fact!

Feelings of disgust invoke physical responses, including a change in heart rate and a heightened gag reflex. If at any time you feel woozy, nauseated, or just too grossed out while flipping through the book, zip back to this page for an awesome blast of fun overload. Remember, **YOUR HAPPY PLACE** is always here for you. We suggest you bookmark this disgust-free refuge and make frequent rest stops during your grand gross adventure.

CHAPTER 1

Horrible History

WHAT'S CONSIDERED GROSS today might not have been so repulsive yesterday. Think rotten teeth are repulsive? Try telling that to the 16th-century English ladies who blackened their choppers to imitate their yuck-mouthed queen. And good luck explaining to a medieval lord that it's rude to spit gristle on the dining room floor! History books often leave out the details of horrible hygiene and foul professions. This chapter, however, will convince you there really is no better time than the present.

If some wild-haired scientist ever invites you to explore the past in a time machine, don't forget to pack nose plugs! Bad breath, body odor, and the stench of poo piled willy-nilly all combined to create a funky fog that stunk up the ages. Hold your nose as we make two stops in the putrid past.

HISTORY *Stinks*

Ancient Egypt (1500 B.C.)

You can't fault the ancient Egyptians for smelling less than fresh. After toiling in the fields or slaving away on monumental construction sites in the desert heat, they had to brave bathing in the Nile River and its canals, home to hungry crocodiles, ornery hippos, and parasites that flourished in the floating sewage. Only royalty and the rich scrubbed in bathtubs. They used a primitive soap made from a salty substance known as natron—a key ingredient in the mummy-making process!

Typical ancient Egyptian villages had narrow streets splattered with donkey poop and cluttered with garbage. Dogs lifted their legs on doorways, while cats treated each village like a giant litter box. Now add the aroma of human waste piling up in primitive toilets (usually a box of sand placed under a stone seat) and take a whiff at high noon in the desert heat. It's no surprise that villagers burned incense to mask foul smells!

Medieval Europe (A.D. 1300)

You'd likely wrinkle your nose even before crossing the drawbridge of a 13th-century European castle. Sewage from the garderobes—or bathrooms—floated in the moat. Roaming livestock and the castle stables made the main courtyard smell like a zoo. In the great hall, where the lord and lady ate and entertained, diners fed scraps to begging dogs that did their business under the tables.

The lord and lady traveled with their own bathtubs, but they rarely used them. Queen Elizabeth I boasted that she bathed once a month, "whether she needed it or not." Knights leaving the battlefield or tournament grounds would have been especially aromatic. Their armor was too cumbersome to accommodate bathroom breaks, so they answered nature's call from the saddle. Imagine the job of the poor squire who had to scour mud, blood, and doo-doo from his master's armor using nothing but vinegar-soaked sand!

HISTORIC SCENT STOPPERS

PERFUME: To cover their stench, ancient Egyptians wore wigs scented with sweet-smelling goop and used deodorants mixed from incense, lettuce, fruit, and myrrh.

BATHHOUSES: Two thousand years ago, citizens of the Roman Empire scrubbed daily in elaborate public baths. After the empire's fall, bathing was beyond the means of most people—and was even considered sinful and unhealthy!

NOSEGAYS: North America's 18th-century colonists buried their noses in scented kerchiefs to block the sweaty stench of their unwashed neighbors.

A TOILET TIME LINE

Potty Spotting

WE TRACE THE EVOLUTION OF THE BEST SEAT IN THE HOUSE

3000 B.C.

STONE AGE DRAINAGE

The first in-home toilets are developed 5,000 years ago in Skara Brae, a small settlement on a chilly Scottish island. Holes in each stone hut lead to smelly drains that carry the waste away—if not the poopy smell. Hey, it beats going out in the cold!

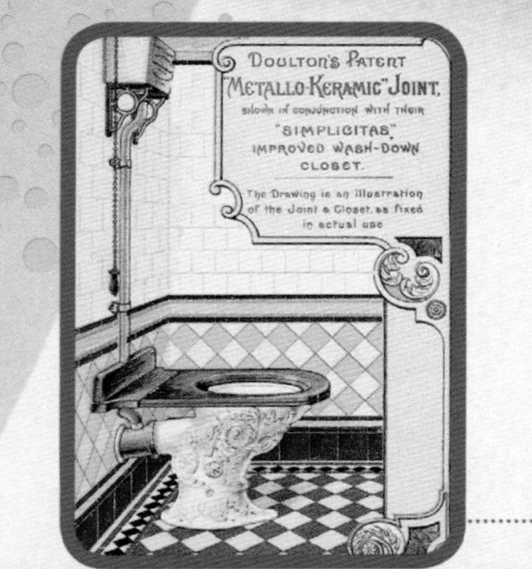

A.D. 1596

SIR JOHN'S "JOHN"

Englishman Sir John Harington invents a new type of flushable "water closet" for his home. His powerful godmother—Queen Elizabeth I—installs one in her palace, but Harington's invention goes unnoticed for 200 years, until a Scottish watchmaker named Alexander Cummings invents a pipe that blocks stinky sewer odors.

1700 B.C.

QUEEN'S THRONE

Knossos Palace on the Greek island of Crete is home to history's first-known flush toilet. Built for the queen, it has a wooden seat set over a drain flushed with water poured through earthenware pipes.

A.D. 200

TOILET FOR TEN

Roman citizens do their business side by side on benchlike toilets that empty into an elaborate sewer system. They even share a sponge-tipped stick for wiping! Toilet technology goes down the drain after the fall of the Roman Empire. For the next 1,700 years, most people poop and pee in "chamber pots" they empty out the window.

A.D. 1200

HOLE IN THE WALL

People living in castles relieve themselves in the garderobe: a hole cut into a stone bench over a shaft that empties into the moat or a latrine pit. Lords and ladies wipe with scratchy hay.

A.D. 1884

CRAPPER'S TOILETS

English plumber Thomas Crapper perfects flush-toilet technology at a time when indoor plumbing becomes more common in Europe and the United States. Crapper's improvements bring toilets into the mainstream. Toilet paper also comes into popular use around this time.

FLUSH FORWARD

FUTURISTIC FLUSHING

Japan takes the lead in toilet technology with seats that spray water, eliminating the need for wiping. Later models come with heaters (no more cold seats!) and even make bubbling sounds to disguise any, er ... natural noises. Today, Japan reigns as the world's leader in toilet comfort.

DARYL THE DUNG BEETLE'S FOUL FACTS

A SOLID GOLD TOILET on display in Hong Kong is worth roughly **$37 million.**

IF YOU CAUGHT A FEVER in ancient China, your doctor would have prescribed hot earthworm soup. In a medieval castle—where your barber doubled as your surgeon—a typical medical treatment involved being bled to the point of dizziness. European doctors in the 16th century crafted cures from ground-up mummy.

It's tough to tell what was worse in the days before modern medicine: getting sick or getting healed. Consider these other nasty treatments prescribed throughout the ages...

BAD MEDICINE

THE AILMENT: Eye irritation
THE PLACE: ancient Egypt
THE DATE: 2000 B.C.
THE TREATMENT: Sweet-and-sour goop!
Priests applied an ointment of honey mixed with human brains—and maybe a little animal poop—to the eye. Fortunately, the eye makeup fancied by men and women of the time also fought infection.

THE AILMENT: Infected cut
THE PLACE: Europe
THE DATE: A.D. 1550
THE TREATMENT: Maggots!
These writhing white worms—the larval (or baby) form of flies—were crammed into the wound. The maggots munched all the rotten meat, leaving behind healthy tissue.

MAGGOTS!

POISON!

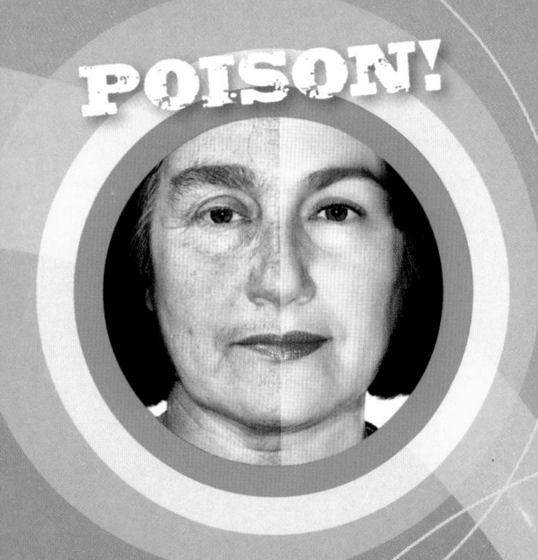

THE AILMENT: Aging
THE PLACE: United States
THE DATE: A.D. 2002-today
THE TREATMENT: Poison!
Men and women unhappy with their wrinkles can seek injections of botulinum—the most potent neurotoxin known to science. (It can cause a lethal food poisoning known as botulism!) Taken in regular "Botox treatments," this toxin helps smooth away the lines of aging. Unfortunately, Botox can also hinder a person's ability to form facial expressions.

SKULL DRILLING!

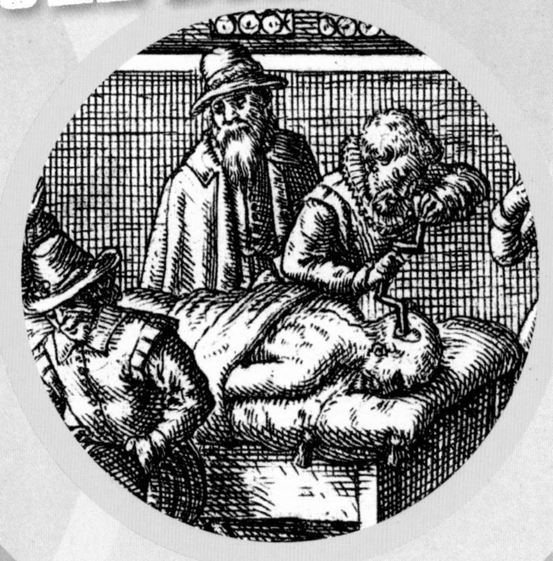

THE AILMENT: Headache
THE PLACE: Peru
THE DATE: 400 B.C.
THE TREATMENT: Skull drilling!
Since ancient times, healers have treated everything from skull fractures to depression by drilling holes in their patients' skulls—a procedure called trephination. Many patients survived this earliest form of brain surgery. They often wore the skull chip around their necks to drive away evil spirits!

THE AILMENT: Fever
THE PLACE: Europe
THE DATE: A.D. 1810
THE TREATMENT: Leeches!
Believing that bleeding helped drain bad blood and restore proper circulation, doctors attached blood-sucking worms to the sick. As many as a hundred leeches might feed off a patient in one session!

LEECHES!

The ancient Egyptians get all the credit for making mummies, but that's hardly fair to the Chinchorro people of ancient Chile. They figured out how to preserve their dead 2,000 years earlier! Many cultures, in fact, left a legacy of creepy corpses. Disengage your gag reflex and you can learn a lot from these far-flung mummies.

BOG BODY

Meet the MUMMiES

BOG BODIES

The murky waters of Europe's peat bogs hold a scary secret. For more than 2,000 years, these foggy swamps have been dumping grounds for executed criminals, murder victims, and human sacrifices. The battered bodies undergo a bizarre preservation process once they slip beneath the surface.Plant-based chemicals in this squishy soup turn skin to leather, dye hair orange, and melt bones into mush. What's left is a leathery bag of boneless skin that retains the body's features right down to fingerprints and beard stubble.

What archaeologists learned: Ancient Europeans had style! Archaeologists found gel made from vegetable oil and tree sap in the hair of one 2,000-year-old bog body. The preserved corpse of another man found nearby had manicured fingernails to die for!

CHINCHORRO PEOPLE OF CHILE

When their people began keeling over from mysterious causes 7,000 years ago, northern Chile's Chinchorro culture disassembled the bodies, yanked out the organs, peeled off the skin, then put everything back together using sticks and reeds. Undiscovered until 1917, these are the world's oldest man-made mummies. The Chinchorro continued their mummy-making tradition for another 3,000 years.

What archaeologists learned: Many had died from drinking water contaminated with a natural poison.

THE BOY KING

The discovery of the tomb of Tutankhamun, aka King Tut, in 1922 ignited a worldwide passion for everything ancient Egypt, but unfortunately the boy king took a beating in the process. Archaeologists cut Tut's 3,300-year-old body into pieces to pry it from the sticky sacred oils that coated the inside of his coffin. Such rough handling inflicted injuries that made it tough to tell what really caused the king's demise. Some archaeologists suspected that he had been murdered!

What archaeologists learned: Recent DNA testing revealed that the teenage king was sickly and likely died of infection from a busted leg rather than foul play.

FRIENDLY GHOSTS

Shriveled mummies perch on a cliff face overlooking the jungle village of the Anga people in Papua New Guinea, but the villagers aren't afraid. Instead, they treat these ghastly guardians—the skin-and-bone bodies of respected ancestors—as if they were still among the living. They even involve the mummies in village activities! Mummification has fallen out of fashion in the region, but the Anga chief wants to resume the tradition, starting with his own body. When he dies, his son will cram a bamboo tube into his backside to drain his body's fluids. Next, the chief's body will sit in a smoke-filled hut until his flesh withers like beef jerky. Once dried out and preserved, he will join his ancestors on the cliff wall.

What archaeologists learned: American mummy expert Ronald Beckett got a hands-on lesson in preserving the dead. The Anga tribe invited him to spruce up the tattered bodies of their beloved ancestors.

HOW TO MAKE A MUMMY

For the people of ancient Egypt, death was just the beginning of an eternal adventure. But gaining entry into the afterlife wasn't as easy as tumbling off a pyramid. The Egyptians believed the spirits of their dearly departed would wither without access to their former bodies, so priests perfected the process of mummification to keep corpses from rotting away. Here's the 4,000-year-old formula in four grisly steps . . .

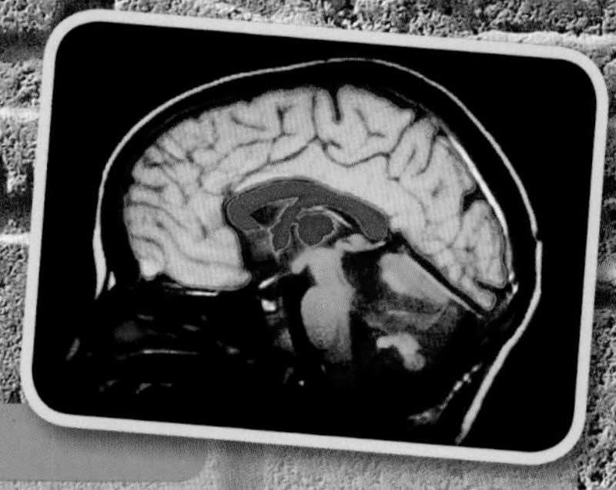

Step 1

DRAIN THE BRAIN

The mummy makers carry each corpse to a sacred tent deep in the desert, where the body is washed and laid on a special table. A priest crams an iron hook up the dead person's nose, swirling it like an eggbeater to mash the brain into gooey bits. Considered useless, the liquefied brain is dumped in the trash. Next time you see a scary mummy in a horror movie, remember: It's brainless!

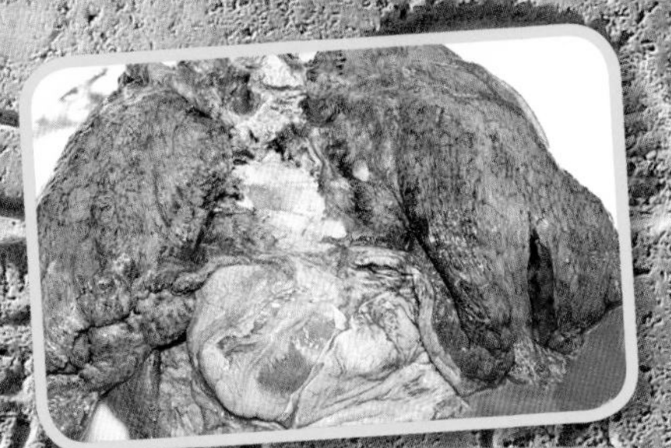

Step 2

ORGANIZE THE ORGANS

Another priest makes a long slice in the body and yanks out all the organs. The liver, stomach, intestines, and lungs are all cleaned, preserved, and sealed in special "canopic jars" carved to look like the gods who guard these organs. The heart—considered crucial equipment for the perilous journey through the underworld—is kept in place.

Step 3

DRYING TIME

Priests pack the body cavity with an Egyptian salt called natron that sops up all the moisture. More natron is piled on top of the corpse, which is left to dry for 40 days. (Less well-to-do Egyptians get the budget treatment, which lasts just a week.) The natron is then scooped away, and the body is filled with spices, rags, and plants so it doesn't look like a deflated flesh balloon.

DARYL THE DUNG BEETLE'S FOUL FACTS

THE ANCIENT EGYPTIANS mummified animals as well as people. Archaeologists have discovered mummies of cats, dogs, donkeys, hawks, crocodiles—even lions!

Step 4

THAT'S A WRAP

Priests rub the corpse's skin with oils and resins to soften it. (Modern scientists discovered that these substances repel bacteria that would decompose the body.) Layers of linen, treated with the same oils, are wrapped around the mummy, giving it the famous bandaged look seen in movies. Finally, the priests tuck magical amulets into the wrappings and utter spells to activate their protective powers. The finished mummy is ready for a happy hereafter.

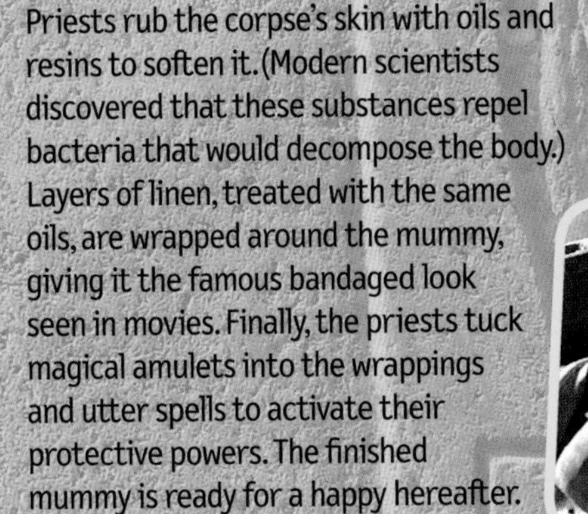

HISTORY'S FIVE NASTIEST CAREERS

Next time you have to change your baby brother's poopy diaper, consider this: At least wiping smelly butts isn't your full-time job! Pity the poor people stuck with these cruel careers.

ODOR TESTER

5 When modern cosmetics and food companies need to know if their products stink, they hire professional smellers to take a whiff. Odor testers stick their noses in a lot of places—from vats of packaged food to stinky armpits while testing deodorant.

GROOM OF THE STOOL

4 How good is it to be the king? Get this: his highness had his own heiney-wiper. It was the groom's number-one mission to cleanse the king after he went number two. As nasty as it sounds, groom of the stool was a highly prized appointment in 16th century England.

LEECH COLLECTOR

3 Healers from the Middle Ages through the 19th century paid handsomely for leeches, but that didn't make the job of gathering these bloodsuckers any less ghastly. Collectors waded through worm-infested waters, using their bare legs as bait. Infection was a common on-the-job hazard.

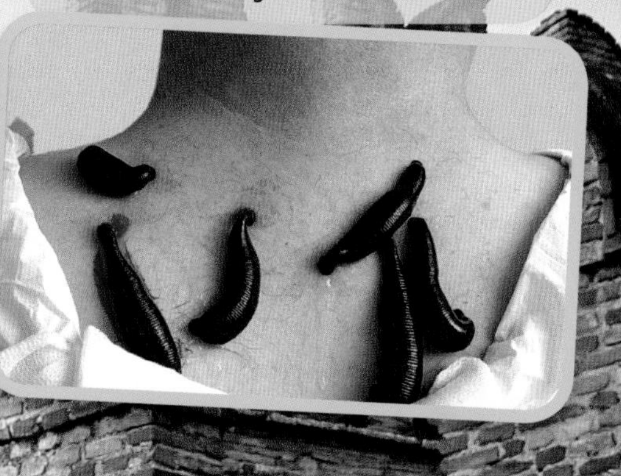

SEARCHER OF THE DEAD

2 One out of every six Londoners died from the bubonic plague in 1665. Searchers of the dead had the grim job of going door to door and carting away the corpses, risking infection from the "Black Death" at each stop.

GONG FARMER

1 Charged with cleaning the cesspits beneath castle garderobes and 16th century homes in Europe, the gong farmer was a human pooper scooper. The job paid well, but hard-working farmers often found themselves up to their necks in doo-doo. Some even suffocated from the foul fumes!

WHO'S FOR DINNER?

Here's a Hint: It's **NOT** Chicken!

IT'S A SCENE RIGHT OUT OF A SILLY OLD MOVIE: Two inept explorers lose their way in the jungle and suddenly find themselves in hot water—literally! Prodded at spearpoint by fearsome tribal warriors, the confused explorers climb into a cauldron of broth flavored with bobbing carrot slices and minced onion. As the village chief fans the flames beneath the cauldron, the two men come to grips with their horrible fate: They're about to become explorer soup!

This Hollywood predicament is actually rooted in reality. Since prehistoric times, people have eaten people—a worldwide practice known as cannibalism. Cannibals didn't boil their victims alive in cauldrons the size of hot tubs like in the movies. They prepared their prey just like they did any animal-based dish. Victims were skinned and roasted. Bones were split to remove the tasty marrow. Skulls were boiled and cracked like coconuts for their protein-rich brains. Cannibals steamed human flesh in palm leaves, added spongy bits of bone to soups, and simmered fat in stews of beans and corn. Humans and their ancestors have been eating each other for at least 800,000 years, so the recipes for our flesh are likely endless!

While hunger drove our Neanderthal ancestors—along with survivors of air and sea disasters and stranded explorers—to nibble on one another, other cases of cannibalism arose for all kinds of cultural reasons. The ancient Xiximes of northern Mexico believed that devouring their enemies would guarantee a bountiful harvest. Hunters of many cultures munched on morsels of their dearly departed to absorb their stalking skills. Warriors of the fierce Maori culture in New Zealand would eat fallen foes as a sort of ultimate insult. (What could be more disrespectful, after all, than turning your enemy into dinner?)

Which really only leaves one question: Are humans really that delicious? According to research, people meat has a flavor similar to pork. Now there's a fun fact you can share at your next barbecue.

HOW THEY SHRANK HEADS!

Of all the world's head-hunting tribes, only the Jivaro clan of Peru and Ecuador shrank their prizes to a convenient souvenir size! Here's how they minimized noggins...

STEP 1 Hack off the victim's head in battle.

STEP 2 Slit the skin of the head from the back of the neck to the crown. Yank it off the skull, hair and all, like a rubber mask.

STEP 3 Sew up the slit in the skin, along with the mouth and eye holes. Dip the entire sticky mess into vegetable extract to stave off smelly rot.

STEP 4 Fill the head with hot sand or rocks and rotate it so it dries evenly. Replace the sand once it cools. Within a few days, the head will have shrunk to the size of a fist. Ta-da! The world's most horrible keychain is ready!

DARYL THE DUNG BEETLE'S FOUL FACTS

UP UNTIL 2006, wannabe cannibals could have sampled Hufu, a **TOFU-BASED NOVELTY FOOD** with the texture and flavor of human flesh.

GROSS GRUDGE MATCH

Roman Feast vs.

A THOUSAND YEARS separate the toga-clad citizens of the Roman Empire from the lords and ladies of medieval Europe, but the powerful people of both periods had one thing in common: They knew how to party! Kings and their barons dined with knights and nobles in rowdy castle halls. Roman aristocrats practically filled their bellies to bursting at frequent festivals—and then made room for more. Who had the fouler feast? Here's a hint: Only one group partied till they puked.

The SETTING

Ancient Rome: There was nothing nasty about the posh villas where well-to-do Romans wined and dined. Revelers reclined on comfy couches around a table piled with exotic dishes, while slaves on the sidelines saw to every guest's whim. And because Roman citizens scrubbed in bathhouses, everyone at the table could actually smell their food—not just each other's armpit odor.

Medieval castle: In the great hall, diners sat at long tables while servers carried mounds of food from the kitchens. Begging dogs wandered the hall and lifted their legs on the benches. Animal poop and food scraps littered the floor, attracting bugs and rodents. Instead of sweeping it up, servants scattered leaves and dried flowers over the whole mess, giving the great hall a not-so-great aroma.

The TABLE MANNERS

Ancient Rome: Diners were expected to lie on their sides facing the table, with one hand propping up their heads. They used the fingers of their other hand to eat. It was considered impolite to use the ring and pinky fingers.

Medieval castle: The lord, lady, and their guests often drank from the same cup and dug into shared dishes with greasy hands (forks hadn't been

Medieval Banquet

The MOST GROSS ROMAN FEAST!

Romans may have had finer foods and better hygiene, but just think about the poor slaves who had to mop up all the throw-up left on the floor after each feast!

Medieval castle: Belching was considered perfectly appropriate at the lord's table, as long as diners didn't burp directly at their neighbors.

Ancient Rome: Romans were infamous for feasting until they could feast no more—and then spewing on the floor to make room for seconds, and thirds, and fifths.

The BODILY FUNCTIONS

Medieval castle: For extra-special occasions, the cooks prepared peacocks sautéed in their feathers, roasted porpoise, or fried stork, all washed down with wine and a low-alcoholic beverage called small beer—even the children drank it!

invented). Spitting bones and gristle on the table was a no-no; spitting on the floor was A-OK! Don't try that at home.

The DELICACIES

Ancient Rome: Ancient Romans were big fans of dormouse, a ratty rodent they raised just for eating. A typical dormouse dish called for pork stuffing and a honey glaze. Snails were another delicacy. Every meal was accompanied with lots of watered-down wine.

History's Worst Firsts

FIRST PERSON TO WHIZ ON THE MOON!

Date: July 20, 1969

Original moonwalker Neil Armstrong may have made history with his "one small step for man," but his fellow Apollo 11 astronaut Buzz Aldrin was the first person to take one giant leak for mankind. Aldrin did his business into a special pee bag built into his space suit while bounding across the lunar surface.

FIRST MAN MUMMIFIED BY MOTHER NATURE!

Date: 3300 B.C.

Despite his shriveled, see-through skin and rotted facial features, Ötzi the Iceman actually looks great for his age. His body is 5,300 years old! Preserved by the cold, dry climate of the Alpine region where he was discovered in 1991, Ötzi is the world's oldest natural mummy. Scientists studying his tattooed body discovered that he was murdered by an arrow to the back. The identity and motives of his Copper Age killer, however, are lost to the mists of time.

FIRST PERSON TO CAN HIS POOP!

Date: May 1961

When he filled 90 tins with his own feces, Italian artist Piero Manzoni planned to sell each can for its weight in gold. Thirty years later, one can sold at auction for nearly $70,000! Art collectors debate whether Manzoni truly pooped in his cans or just filled them with worthless plaster, but no one has broken out a can opener to find out.

FIRST FAMOUS PROFESSIONAL TOOTER!

Date: 1887

Tooting is art for the flatulist, a type of entertainer who passes gas on command. The most famous of all was Joseph Pujol. This 19th-century French "fartomaniac" entertained royalty with his tooting abilities, which included imitating thunderstorms and "playing the flute." Here's hoping no one tried playing that flute the normal way after one of Pujol's performances.

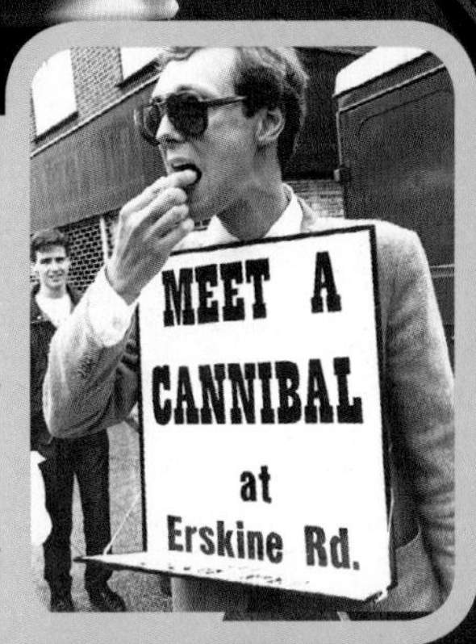

FIRST PERSON TO EAT PEOPLE AS ART!

Date: July 19, 1988

Rick Gibson—an artist with an appetite for the outrageous—was far from repulsed when a pal gave him a bottle of preserved human tonsils. Instead, he decided to devour the meatball-size organs on a London sidewalk, becoming the first street-corner cannibal in British history.

SQUEAKY CLEAN

According to one study, today's kids on average bathe **EVERY DAY** of the week.

STINKY QUEEN

Queen Isabella of Castile claimed she only bathed **TWICE** in her life. Fortunately for her husband, one of those times was right before her wedding.

LIFE EXPECTANCY THROUGH THE AGES

Stone Age (10,000 B.C.): 20 years

Ancient Greece (500 B.C.): 28 years

Medieval Europe (A.D. 1200): 31 years

Today: 78 years

Horrible HISTORY LESSON

GAG GAUGE

DiRTY JOBS

Daryl the Dung Beetle Ranks History's **NASTIEST CAREERS**

Job	Gag Gauge
Gong Farmer	BLAAARGH!
Groom of the Stool	
Searcher of the Dead	SICKENING
Leech Collector	
Odor Tester	UNSETTLING

CHAPTER 2

Your Abominable Body

YOU CAME INTO THIS WORLD slathered in blood and covered in goo. Then things really got nasty! A fountain of foul substances, the human body is a walking, talking, gas factory and an unstoppable producer of poop. Over an average lifetime, it will churn out seas of snot and puddles of pus. Oh, yeah—and it smells bad, too! Plunge ahead to see why human anatomy is so good at being grody.

GERMS!

DON'T PANIC, but you're outnumbered by alien life-forms! They look like hairy hot dogs, spiky blobs, and oozing spirals, and they're crawling across—and deep inside—your body right now. They're bacteria!

Your body is built of trillions of itty-bitty living blobs, called cells, that work together to do amazing things, such as holding in your organs or beating your brother at *Super Mario Kart*. But for every cell you call your own, ten foreign bacteria can be found clustering around or near it. You can't see these hideous hitchhikers, but you can certainly smell them. Like any living thing, bacteria eat, reproduce, die, and create waste. This waste is the source of your body odor, bad breath, and torturous toots. In other words, bacteria make your life stink!

Scientists call these communities of foreign bacteria your body's "flora," and no two people host the same mix of microorganisms. If the thought of serving as a human-shaped planet for microscopic inhabitants makes you queasy, relax: Most of your body's microbes are essential for good health. In fact, scientists are beginning to think of your flora as just another organ. That doesn't make bacteria any less disgusting. Viruses and other microbial meanies—aka germs—trigger some of your body's most repulsive reactions.

GERMS!

Little Monsters

Meet four famous bacteria that call your body home sweet home . . .

ESCHERICHIA COLI

This rod-shaped microbe lives deep in your guts, the body's busiest bacterial neighborhood. Helpful E. coli strains produce an important vitamin. Harmful ones make you puke for days.

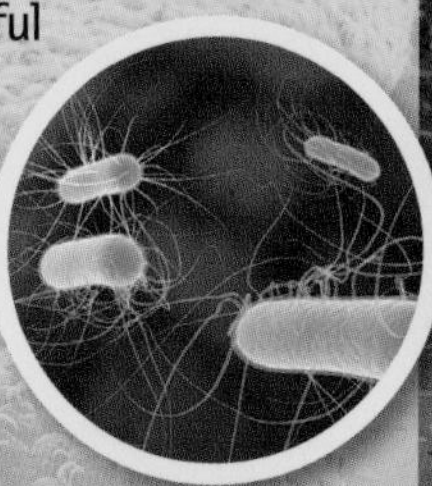

BREVIBACTERIUM LINENS

This foul-smelling microbe thrives in the sweat simmering in your sneakers, unleashing an awful stink when you kick off your shoes. It's also used to ferment stinky Limburger cheese.

ACTINOMYCES VISCOSUS

When your dentist breaks out the power tools to jackhammer the brownish coat of slime known as plaque from your teeth, he's actually attacking these mouth-dwelling bacteria.

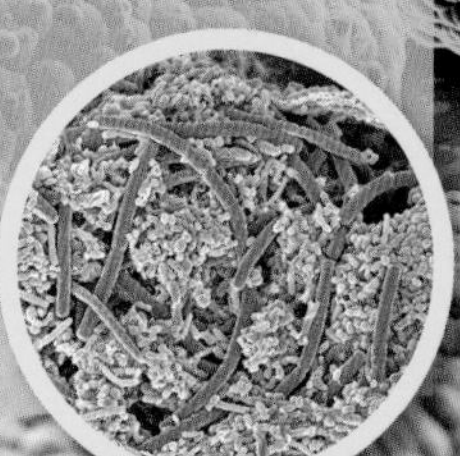

METHANOGENS

About half of all people have these super-simple microbes living in their guts. Methanogens produce methane, a greenhouse gas that animals pass into the atmosphere when they poot.

DARYL THE DUNG BEETLE'S FOUL FACTS

BELLY-BUTTON LINT—a mix of clothing fibers and dead skin cells—is a breeding ground for bacteria. Scientists recently discovered more than **600 NEW SPECIES** of microbes living in people's navels!

Magical Mucus

IT'S THE KIND OF ALL-PURPOSE PRODUCT YOU'D EXPECT TO SEE ADVERTISED ON A TV INFOMERCIAL. Ladies and gentlemen, meet mucus! Available in many fashionable colors (green, yellow, and even brown) this slimy mix of water and germ-killing chemicals has a million and one uses—all of them disgusting!

You don't need to act now to order mucus from TV; specialized tissues in your lungs, stomach, intestines, and elsewhere produce buckets of the stuff for free. What does your body do with all that goop? Behold, the uses of mucus!

IT'S THE SOURCE OF ALL SNOT!

Mucus goes by many nicknames, and "snot" is the unscientific term used to describe nasal mucus. It serves as your first line of defense against germs, dust, and pollen particles that would impede breathing if they reached your lungs. Moved along by tiny nostril hairs called cilia, snot pummels and pushes invading particles toward the exit—your nostrils—or dumps them down your throat.

IT'S A COLD KILLER!

Your nasal membranes produce nearly two gallons (seven liters) of mucus each week, but you usually swallow all that snot without giving it a second thought. Catch a cold virus or come under an allergy attack, however, and the membranes pump up the volume. Your nose turns into a leaky snot faucet. You start coughing up globs of phlegm—a type of mucus produced in your throat and lungs. A hacking cough and runny nose are your body's ways of flushing out all the bad stuff.

IT'S A BOOGER BUILDER!

Snot is sticky for a reason—it collects all the crud that blows up your nose. Once snot reaches the nostrils, it dries into crumbly little boogers for easy disposal. Polite people blow them into tissues; everyone else engages in rhinotillexis, the technical term for nose-picking. Just so you know, most doctors advise against devouring your diggings.

IT'S A STOMACH SAVER!

You should be happy that your stomach is inside your body and not the other way around. Your belly drips with an acid strong enough to dissolve metal. This corrosive bath obliterates harmful bacteria and liquefies your food, but what keeps it from burning through your guts? By now you should know the answer: mucus! A constantly replenishing layer lines the stomach, keeping it from eating itself.

IT'S AN ORGAN GREASER!

Drive a car without oil and its engine will soon overheat and shut down. Your body is no different. Organs need lubrication to run smoothly and for protection from germs and particles. Just be glad you don't produce mucus on the outside of your body, like a certain sea creature you'll learn about soon enough.

NOT SNOT, BUT STILL NASTY...

SALIVA: Also known as spit, this watery substance flows from glands in the mouth to moisten your food, kill bacteria, and protect your throat from stomach acid when you barf.

SWEAT: Odorless until it's tainted by bacteria, sweat is secreted from glands in your skin to cool your body and flush away waste.

PUS: This thick, yellowish ooze collects in pimples and other points of inflammation. It's a mix of bacteria, dead skin, and dead white blood cells that gave their lives fighting infection.

Wee Will Rock You

TAKE A MOMENT TO STAND UP, SQUEEZE YOUR THIGHS TOGETHER, AND BEND AT THE WAIST. Now, hop back and forth! Feel familiar? You're doing the pee-pee dance, and everyone who's experienced that special sense of urgency knows the moves. It's an international sensation!

But before you can hit the dance floor—and the bathroom—several processes in your body need to fill your tank. Unlike poop, urine (aka, pee) doesn't begin its journey in your stomach. The flow begins in a twin set of organs located in the small of your back...

1 MAGIC BEANS

The kidney is such an important organ, your body comes with two of them! (One can do all the work if the other breaks down.) Each of these bean-shaped organs is crammed with more than a million microscopic filters—called nephrons—that skim the waste chemicals and other gunk from your blood. Where does that waste come from? All over your body! Blood is constantly carrying nutrients to your organs and flushing away waste chemicals and other junk. All that bad stuff, along with any excess fluid, is drained into special tubes called ureters.

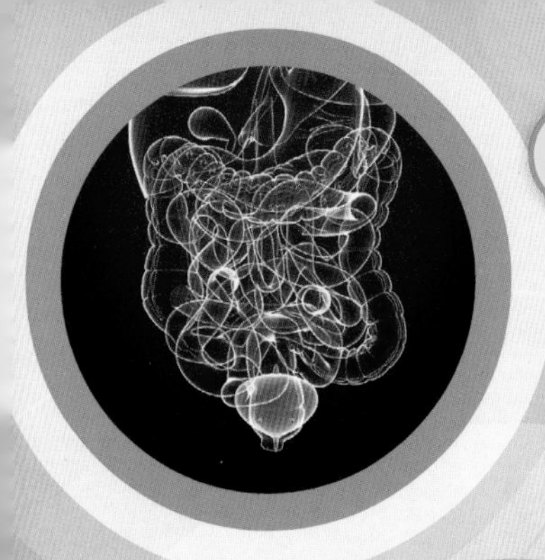

2 BLADDER UP

The ureters connect to a stretchy pouch called the bladder. As the bladder fills, it balloons in size until it reaches capacity—about a pint (473 ml) of fluid. A full bladder sends your brain into yellow alert. The mounting pressure has you scrambling for the nearest bathroom (while you do your darndest not to think about waterfalls and tidal waves).

3 GO TIME!

Once you finally find the appropriate pee receptacle—a toilet, a tree, or (worst-case scenario) a Porta-Potty—your bladder opens its exit valve and empties through your urethral opening. Sterile when it exits your body, urine is made of water, urea (a waste product also found in sweat), salts, and other waste chemicals. Bile in your body gives pee its light-yellow color, which becomes darker if you're thirsty. Urine turns reddish if you eat beets or blackberries. Gobbling down asparagus can make your pee extra smelly.

Sorry...
NO
RESTROOMS

THE HAZARDS OF HOLDING IT

Next time you try to sit through a movie without giving your bladder a break, consider the fate of Danish astronomer Tycho Brahe. Out of an ironclad sense of politeness, he refused to visit the loo during an especially long banquet in 1601. When he died days later, doctors believed it was from a burst bladder. His body had slowly drowned in its own pee! (Modern scientists suspect Brahe died of mercury poisoning, but why take a chance with a long pee-pee dance? Let go with the flow!)

The MANY Uses of URiNE

IT'S A BATTERY: Scientists in Singapore invented a way to generate power from pee.

IT'S AN EXPLOSIVE: Saltpeter—a mix of pee and animal poop—is a key component of gunpowder.

IT'S A CLEANER: Bacteria transform the urea in your pee into ammonia, which gives surfaces a streak-free shine.

IT'S A HEALTH DRINK: People have been drinking their own dribbles for centuries. Pee-swiggers swear it boosts their immune systems and even cures cancer!

THE SCOOP ON POOP

POOP HAPPENS. All creatures do it, from submarine-size blue whales to microscopic bacteria. Anything that eats must excrete, and no advancements in medical science will relieve you of your duty to ... make doodie (known as "feces" or "stool" in polite conversation).

But just how does that tasty cheeseburger you devoured yesterday end up as a smelly brown log in your toilet today? Follow along as we trace the origin of your feces.

STAGE 1

GREAT BALLS OF BOLUS

Your body starts digesting dinner the moment you open your mouth. Chemicals in your saliva help melt chewed food into slimy gobs of mush—each called a bolus—for easier swallowing. Your tongue herds each bolus to the back of your throat and drops it into your esophagus, a pipe ringed with muscles that squeeze everything you swallow to your stomach.

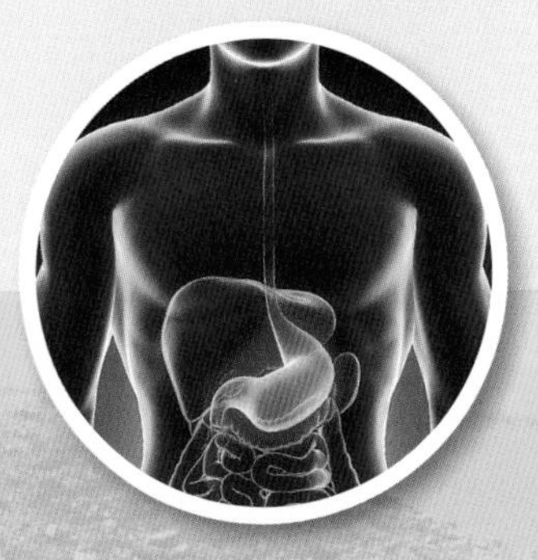

STAGE 2

CHYME TIME

Ever hear someone brag about having an iron stomach? Actually, everyone's stomach is strong! This J-shaped organ—which can expand to accommodate a turkey drumstick, a pile of mashed potatoes, and a slice of pumpkin pie—is lined with mighty muscles that pummel your food. A storm of gastric juices, meanwhile, dissolves your dinner into a thick paste called chyme (pronounced "kime").

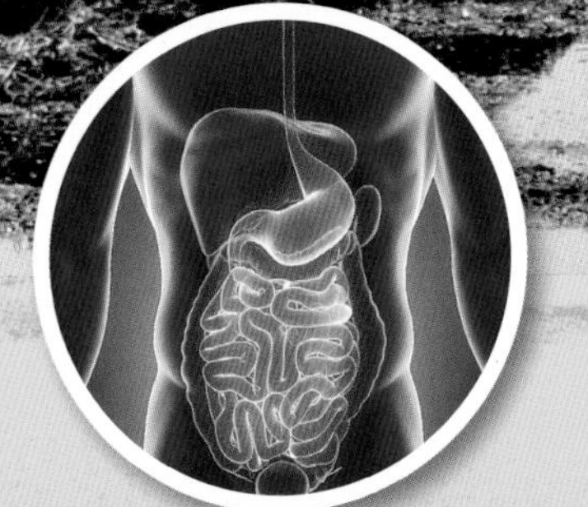

STAGE 3

OUT WITH THE GOOD

Officially poop-in-waiting, chyme dribbles slowly to its next port of call—the small intestine—where the bulk of digestion takes place. This 20-foot (6-m) tube coils through your abdomen and teams with other organs (along with colonies of bacteria) to absorb nutrients from everything you eat. It's followed by the large intestine, which sops up chyme's excess water and minerals.

STAGE 4

A ROUND IN THE CHAMBER

Congratulations! Your meal is now a dry mass of indigestible fiber and dead bacteria, the source of excrement's eye-watering odor. Your poop is about a third the size of whatever you ate, and it's colored brown from waste iron and dead blood cells. When enough feces has reached your rectum—the launch chamber of the digestive system—you start to get that pressing feeling.

DANDRUFF ISN'T DANDY

Castaway skin cells atop your scalp collide and cluster in your hair like little snowballs until they finally dislodge in a blizzard of dead epidermis (the scientific name for your skin's outer layer).

STINK CENTRAL

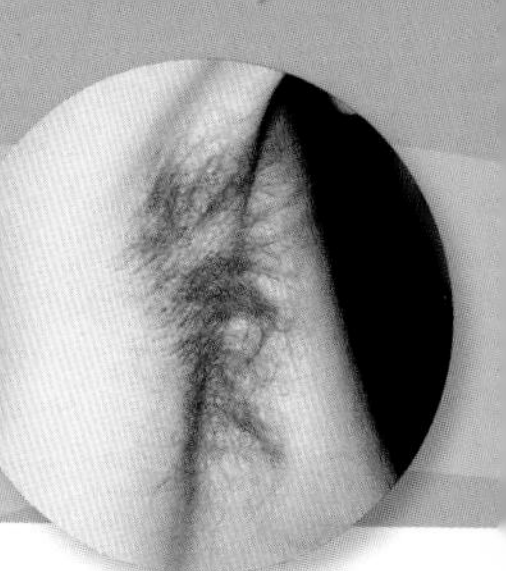

Glands in your skin produce sweat to cool your body and flush out waste. All these secretions are a banquet for bacteria, which produce stinky micro-poop—hence, body odor!

BREATH OF DEATH

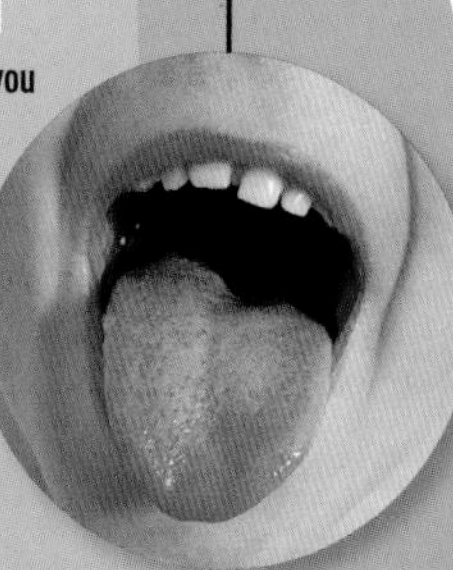

Last night's meat loaf left you with morning breath that could peel paint. Blame the microbes in your mouth. They made a midnight snack of the stuck-on leftovers, raising a royal stink with their secretions.

POP GOES THE PIMPLE

Millions of hair follicles cover your body and produce protective oils, but it takes just one clog to create a zit. Bacteria and oils combine into a repulsive pus that erupts when you give the pimple a squeeze.

Next time you dawdle in the bathroom to admire your pretty skin and shiny hair, beware: Objects in the mirror are grosser than they appear. See for yourself in this head-to-toe tour of your body's disgusting details.

YOU ARE

NATURE'S NASTY BAND-AID

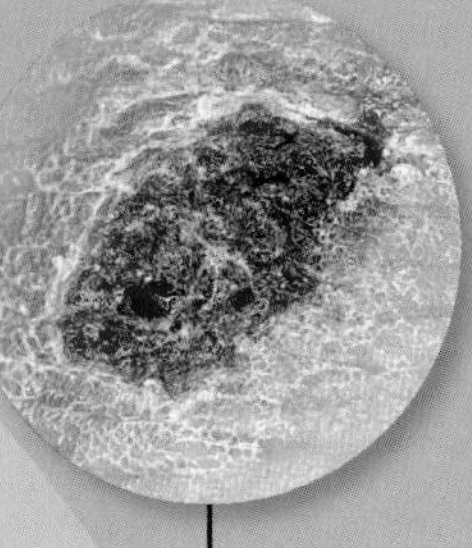

As soon as you suffer a scrape, cells in your blood rush to the wound and seal it. Eventually, this clot dries and hardens into a crusty protective scab. Resist the urge to pick it and fling it at your sister!

TERRIBLE TOES

Your sweaty gym sock is like a five-star spa for fungus, which squeezes under your toenails and causes a burning itch. Between your toes, bacteria combines with lint to create a smelly cheese called toe jam.

DEAD ON THE OUTSIDE

Your body's biggest organ, skin is made of layers of cells that march to the surface and flake off from friction. The outermost layer is entirely dead. You're like a zombie—except you'd rather eat pizza than people!

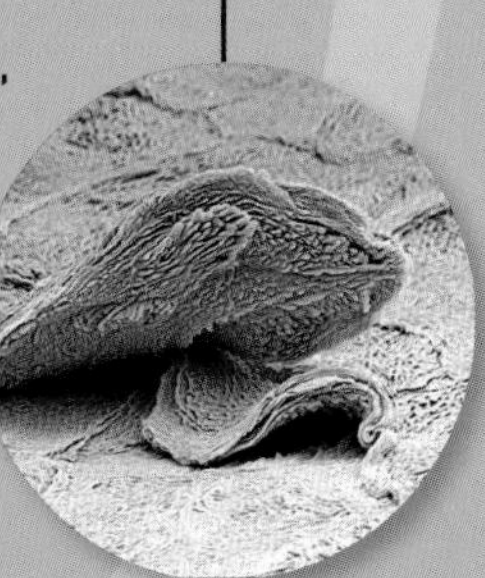

DARYL THE DUNG BEETLE'S FOUL FACTS

FOR EVERY ONE HAIR on your head, there are **6 MILLION MICROBES** in your mouth.

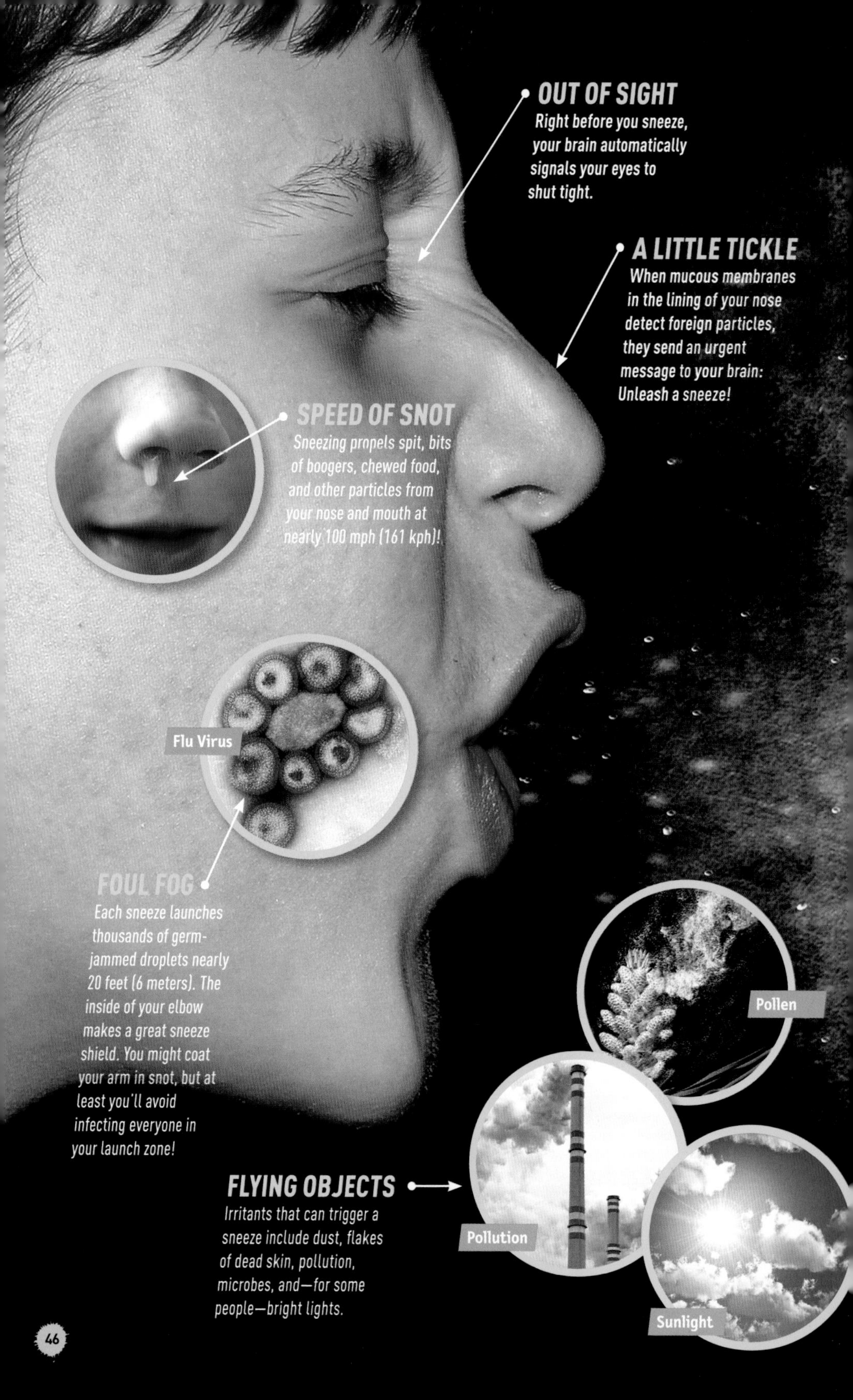

OUT OF SIGHT

Right before you sneeze, your brain automatically signals your eyes to shut tight.

A LITTLE TICKLE

When mucous membranes in the lining of your nose detect foreign particles, they send an urgent message to your brain: Unleash a sneeze!

SPEED OF SNOT

Sneezing propels spit, bits of boogers, chewed food, and other particles from your nose and mouth at nearly 100 mph (161 kph)!

FOUL FOG

Each sneeze launches thousands of germ-jammed droplets nearly 20 feet (6 meters). The inside of your elbow makes a great sneeze shield. You might coat your arm in snot, but at least you'll avoid infecting everyone in your launch zone!

FLYING OBJECTS

Irritants that can trigger a sneeze include dust, flakes of dead skin, pollution, microbes, and—for some people—bright lights.

You can stifle a yawn, hold back a burp, and suppress a giggle, but there's no stopping a sneeze. Lightning-fast involuntary reactions, sneezes occur when your chest, stomach, throat, and face muscles work together to blast foreign particles from your air passages. The whole process lasts less than three seconds, so we've put this force of nature on pause to give it a closer look.

FREEZE THAT Sneeze!

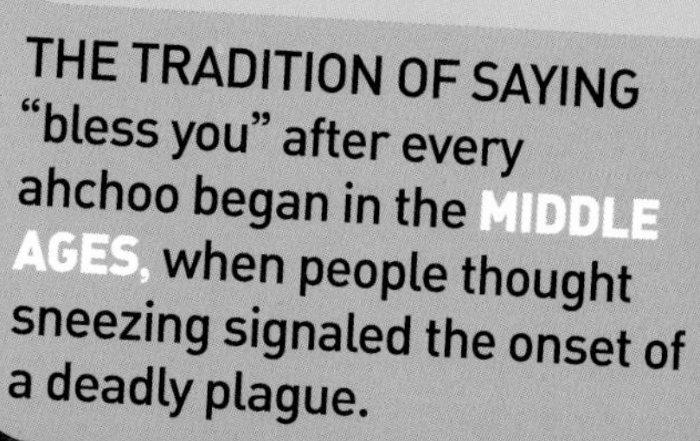

DARYL THE DUNG BEETLE'S FOUL FACTS

THE TRADITION OF SAYING "bless you" after every ahchoo began in the **MIDDLE AGES**, when people thought sneezing signaled the onset of a deadly plague.

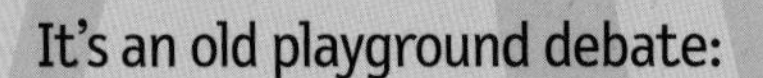

It's an old playground debate:

"Why toot and waste it when you can burp and taste it?" Alas, the decision is out of your hands. Belches and toots spring from different ends of your body, spawned by mostly separate biological processes. Figuring out which bodily function is fouler, however, is simple when you get down to the gross nitty-gritty...

GROSS GRUDGE MATCH

GAS ATTACK

THE CAUSES

HEAD OUT: Every time you eat, drink, talk, chew gum, or yawn, you gulp a bit of air into your stomach. When your belly balloons to its maximum capacity, it releases the bubbles back up your food tube—called your esophagus—and out your mouth and nose.

TAIL END: A small fraction of the gas you pass comes from swallowed air that makes its way to your large intestine, aka your body's toot factory. Here, most of your body's foul fog is pumped out by the billions of bacteria that live in your guts. These microorganisms excrete stinky gas as they help break down tough-to-digest food. They do all the tooting; you take all the blame.

THE SOUNDS

HEAD OUT: Brrraaap! My, what a loud upper esophageal sphincter you have! That's the flexible flap at the tip of your food tube that vibrates as it releases swallowed air from your stomach. The mightiest burp ever recorded was louder than a thunderclap!

TAIL END: Phwooot! Toots fluctuate in volume and timbre—from near-silent squeaks to seat-shaking explosions—depending on how much air is forced through your body's wind instrument: the anal sphincter.

THE FREQUENCY

HEAD OUT: On average, 15 times per day. Increase your frequency by chugging bubbly sodas.

TAIL END: About 14 times each day. Up your flatulence ante by devouring more dairy and wheat products, vegetables, and beans.

THE SMELLS

HEAD OUT: Because they zip through the body faster than toots and are made of nothing but hot air, most belches emerge fragrance-free. Eat a pungent meal, however, and your burps will share the spicy smell. What better way to let everyone know you had pizza rolls for breakfast?

TAIL END: Ninety-nine percent of your flatulence is made of odorless gasses. It's the remaining one percent that puts tears in the eyes of passersby. Food-munching bacteria in your gut produce skatole (the source of poop's stink) and sulfides that infuse toots with that wonderful rotten-egg aroma.

THE MOST GROSS: TAIL END!

Sometimes silent but always violent, toots share the air from your derriere with everyone in your blast radius. Burps, meanwhile, only get the nickel tour of your digestive system. Even the foulest belches smell like a mountain meadow compared to the excremental odors exiting your body's bitter end.

What's Up, Chuck?

The Putrid Truth About Puke

Your stomach churns, your head spins, and your throat begins to burn. Before you know it, blaaargh!!! You've launched your lunch! Vomiting—better known as puking, upchucking, or tossing your cookies—is no picnic! Why would your stomach revolt in such a revolting way? Read on for the lowdown on throw-up.

WHY DO YOU VOMIT?

If you catch the stomach flu (germs or a virus in your guts), swallow food spoiled by bacteria, or simply eat too much of anything, your stomach and intestines will attempt to eject whatever's causing the trouble. Clammy skin, waves of uneasiness, and a queasy feeling known as nausea usually precede vomiting, giving you a heads-up to have a bucket handy. Motion sickness—a condition brought on by winding roads, rocking boats, or back-to-back roller-coaster rides—can cause nausea in some people, leading to vomiting.

WHAT IS PUKE MADE OF?

That lumpy, stinky puddle you spewed (we hope) into a bucket or toilet bowl might not look familiar, but you've actually seen most of it before. It's the chewed, mashed, partially digested pieces of whatever you ate recently, combined with spit, mucus, and perhaps a dash of a digestion-aiding chemical called bile. Bile comes from your intestines and gives vomit its lovely green sheen and grody odor.

IS THERE A WAY TO HOLD BACK FROM BARFING?

Nah, just go with the blow. Although horribly unpleasant, throwing up is usually a good thing. It lets your body eject germs or a disagreeable dinner, and you'll usually feel immediate relief. Sipping water afterward will calm your stomach and wash away the icky taste. If you develop a fever, continue to vomit, or notice a lot of bile in your barf, your parents may consider taking you to the doctor. Motion sickness can be treated with various medications (ask Mom or Dad) or by taking deep, steady breaths of fresh air. Seasickness, however, has only one surefire cure: Land ahoy!

WHY DOES VOMIT BURN YOUR THROAT?

Remember, your stomach contains powerful acids that help break down food, and some of this sour-tasting gastric juice gets pumped up and away when you puke. Although a coating of spit and mucus helps protect your throat and mouth when you vomit, you'll still feel the burn. Particularly forceful barfing sessions will propel puke into your sinuses and out your nose, producing an eye-watering sting. Nasty!

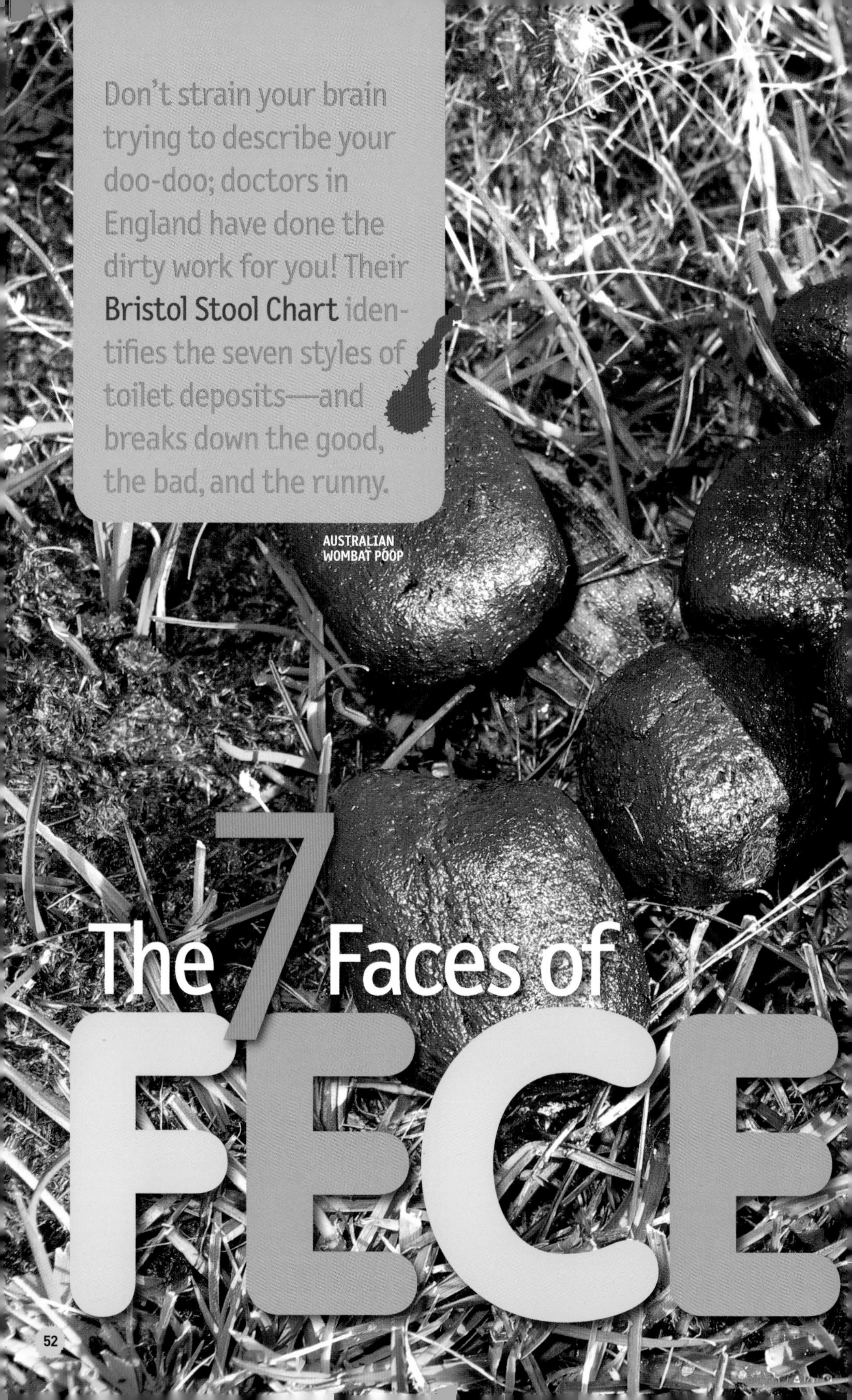

Don't strain your brain trying to describe your doo-doo; doctors in England have done the dirty work for you! Their **Bristol Stool Chart** identifies the seven styles of toilet deposits—and breaks down the good, the bad, and the runny.

AUSTRALIAN WOMBAT POOP

The 7 Faces of FECE

S

TYPE 1

Nut-size lumps that are tough to pass

TYPE 2

Shaped like a hot dog but lumpy like oatmeal

Constipation: Types 1 and 2 are sure signs that your bowels are backed up. Drink more water!

TYPE 3

Shaped like a hot dog, but with a cracked surface

TYPE 4

Smooth like a snake's body, and also soft

TYPE 5

Soft blobs with clear-cut edges. Easy to pass

Healthy poo: These types of poo indicate all is well in your digestive system.

TYPE 6

A mushy goo with fluffy pieces and ragged edges

TYPE 7

Watery, with no solid pieces

Dribbly doo strikes when your body, battling illness, flushes toxins through your digestive tract.

MUCUS MINERS

Nearly **EIGHT PERCENT** of kids pick their noses at least 20 times a day!

FUNKY FEEDERS

TEN PERCENT of kids admit to chewing their own toenails!

SKIN DINERS

FORTY-THREE percent of kids pick off their scabs!

Disgusting STATISTICS

GAG GAUGE

YOUR GROSS BODY

Daryl the Dung Beetle Ranks **UNFORTUNATE AFFLICTIONS.**

Bad Breath

Body Odor

Toe Jam

Pimples

Scabs

Dandruff

BLAAARGH!

SICKENING

UNSETTLING

CHAPTER 3

Nasty Nature

HAUGH...HAUUUGH...HAUUUGHSPLAT!

Any cat owner knows that sickening sound: the squishy launch of an upchucked hair ball! If a cute kitty is capable of such a disgusting bodily function, what horrors might we expect from a snot-covered sea creature called a hagfish? Or the buck-toothed mammal known as the naked mole rat? Mother Nature has an ugly side, which we're about to reveal in all its slimy, gory glory.

SPACE INVADER

The candiru catfish is the Amazon River's number one threat!

A BLOODTHIRSTY MONSTER lurks in the murky waters of the Amazon River. Using fearsome spikes on its head, the creature lodges its skinny body in the gills of fish to feast on their bodily fluids. People who live along the Amazon have come to fear this monster just as much as piranha, bull sharks, and other ferocious freshwater fish. It's a type of catfish called the candiru, and it's only 3 inches (7.6 cm) long.

What's to fear from a fish the size of a crayon? According to legend, candiru catfish occasionally wriggle their way into the bodies of human swimmers—and they do it through the worst opening imaginable. In other words, you should probably never squat to pee in the Amazon River.

Documented cases of candiru attacks on humans are rare and difficult to confirm, particularly because a recent study showed that these catfish aren't attracted to the smell of pee (as was once believed). That hasn't stopped people along the Amazon from taking precautions when swimming in the river. Locals will wear protective clothing and even secure the vulnerable bits of their bodies.

Can you blame them? The candiru's barblike spikes make it difficult to remove without surgery. Once the fish wriggles its way in, good luck getting it out! You're best off taking a bathroom break before getting anywhere near the Amazon River.

PARTNER IN SLIME

THE LAMPREY

With a sleek body like a slimy tube sock, this eel-like fish prowls the depths of rivers, lakes, and oceans looking for creatures it can drill into with its nightmarish mouth of thorny teeth. Once attached, the lamprey slurps blood from its unfortunate host.

AWFUL

ANiMAL AWARDS

MOST PUNGENT PERFUMER

Zorilla

You think a skunk is stinky? It's got nothing on the striped polecat, aka the zorilla, aka smelliest animal on Earth! Like a skunk, this member of the weasel family can squirt a stream of sticky fluid from its butt at any animal that crosses its path. The polecat's spray is almost supernaturally stinky. A ticked-off zorilla was once observed repelling an entire pride of lions from a freshly killed zebra!

MOST MASTERFUL GAS-PASSER

Herring

When people pass gas, everyone nearby cringes (or cracks up, depending on the crowd). When herring toot, all the herring nearby listen intently. That's because this species of fish actually communicates through its flatulence! Scientists studying herring noticed they produced a tootlike "raspberry" sound at night by releasing a stream of bubbles from an opening alongside their butts. Only other herring can hear this high-frequency noise, which helps them cluster in protective schools. Scientists call this sound a Fast Repetitive Tick, or FRT. Silly scientists!

MOST OFFENSIVE DEFENDER

Turkey Vulture

With a featherless face made for digging into maggot-ridden roadkill, turkey vultures are already the uncontested leaders of the dirty-bird club. But you haven't really seen their rotten side until you've ticked one off. These bad birds defend themselves by barfing up whatever decomposing flesh they've recently devoured, along with powerful stomach acids. Lightened of its lunch, the vulture soars to safety while the offending animal wallows in putrid puke.

MOST MONSTROUS MAW

Komodo Dragon

You'd expect the world's largest, heaviest lizard to pack one powerful bite, and you'd be . . . wrong. Despite their size—up to 10 feet (3 meters) long—komodo dragons have wimpy jaws. A house cat has a stronger bite! But these lethal lizards rely on dirty tricks to kill their prey. Their saliva swarms with toxic bacteria, and studies reveal that komodo dragons have venomous mouths just like some snakes. That means each bite delivers a repulsive one-two punch of germs and venom! A dragon rips open prey with its razorlike teeth, then patiently follows the stricken animal until it dies of blood loss or poisoning. Once its yucky mouth has done its dirty work, the lizard moves in for the feast.

MOST DISGUSTING DECORATOR

Hippopotamus

When an African hippo emerges from a local mud hole to mark its territory with poop and pee, it doesn't waste any time spreading its waste. The big beast whips its tail to fan feces and urine in every direction. Scientists aren't certain why hippos spray their excrement to and fro, but they suspect it might serve to attract mates as well as mark territory. Hey, hippos, what's wrong with red roses?

Why Does My Dog Eat Doo?!

And other nasty habits of man's best friend . . .

POOP SNACKING

Nothing's nastier than spotting Spot having his pick of the cat's litter box or dining on his own doodie. Veterinarians suspect that dogs inherited the dookie-devouring instinct from their wolf ancestors. (Mother wolves eat puppy poo to hide the scent of their dens.) Poop-craving canines might also have a diet lacking certain vitamins and enzymes—enzymes they can get from poop.

NIXING THE HABIT: Pooper-scoop your backyard often, scold your pooch for poop-snacking, and be sure to buy kibble that offers a balanced diet.

RUMP RUBBING

If you think it's unsettling to see your dog scoot, scoot, scooting across the living room carpet, wait'll you hear what's causing this behavior: clogged glands. Located next to your pooch's butt, these itty-bitty openings secrete a pungent substance that transmits all kinds of information to other dogs. (That's why pups greet each other by butt-sniffing.) Sometimes these glands get backed up and become itchy, so it's off to the rump races for your dog!

NIXING THE HABIT: Take your poor pooch to the vet for some professional gland handling.

RANCID ROLLING

How many times have you scrubbed Spot clean only to find him frolicking in something yucky the instant he gets outside? A dog's nose is more than a hundred times more sensitive than a human's. And what smells sweet to us might seem overpowering or just plain awful to your pooch, so he'll roll in something smelly to overpower the shampoo odor. Some experts believe dogs instinctively roll in poop or dead critters to disguise their scent or share these foul finds with pack members. Unfortunately in this case, you're part of your dog's pack!

NIXING THE HABIT: Wash your pup with fragrance-free shampoo and keep your yard clean of nasty messes.

Why *Does* My Cat Hack Up That?!

And other bad behaviors of your pretty kitty . . .

HAIR BALL HACKING

Your feline's filthiest habit is actually a side effect of its constant cleanliness. Hey, no fair! Cats groom themselves throughout the day, using their sandpapery tongues to comb food and dirt from their fur. Unfortunately, they gobble down gobs of loose hair with all that gunk. Feline bellies aren't equipped to digest strands of fur, so . . . kersplat! The hair comes out the same way it went in, and you discover soggy sausage-shaped fuzz balls all over the house.

NIXING THE HABIT: Comb your kitty often—especially during shedding season—to get rid of all that excess fur.

PEE SPRAYING

A little squirt behind the house plant. A quick spritz on the couch. Sometimes, it seems like your kitty forgets that the litter box even exists! But your cat isn't relieving itself when it sprays stinky pee around the house. Instead, kitty is claiming territory. Just like dogs, cats live in a 3D world of odors. Squirting urine on furniture or the floor sends other felines a message: "This belongs to me now!"

NIXING THE HABIT: Spaying or neutering your cat while it's young will help stop spraying behavior. Your kitty might also feel threatened or crowded by other cats in the house, so give your felines room to roam alone.

GIFT GIVING

Unless you have a taste for butchered bird or half-minced mouse, you probably don't appreciate the twitching creatures your kitty deposits on your pillow. But trying to stop your cat from hunting and sharing is like asking your sister to quit tooting in her sleep—it's a battle against nature! Biologists think cats share their kills out of motherly instinct. Mama cats bring battered critters to their kittens to teach them hunting skills. Your gift-giving kitty probably thinks your stalking skills are rusty.

NIXING THE HABIT: You'll never curb your cat's killer instinct. If you're sick of receiving grisly gifts, keep kitty inside.

DARYL THE DUNG BEETLE'S FOUL FACTS

SOMETIMES people can develop hair balls—**CALLED BEZOARS**—from habitually chewing on their hair. Medieval Europeans even carried bezoars as good luck charms!

AWW, *Cute!*

Koalas

AWW, CUTE!

With their cotton-ball ears and laid-back lifestyle, these Australian tree-dwelling marsupials look like stuffed animals—especially when they're carrying their babies (called joeys) on their backs or bellies.

OH, YUCK!

A koala joey spends its first six months sipping on pap—a poopy soup made in its mother's intestines. Pap is swarming with bacteria that will help the adult koala digest toxic eucalyptus.

Wolf Pups

AWW, CUTE!

As their older siblings take turns babysitting, young wolves frolic with each other, practice hunting insects, and play tug-of-war with sticks or strips of animal skin.

OH, YUCK!

Puppies aren't showing affection when they lick the muzzles of older pack members. They're asking for leftovers! The adult wolves dutifully vomit bits of their most recent meal, which the pups eagerly lap up. Partially digested moose again? Hooray!

OH, YUCK!

The nasty side of nature's most adorable animals

Llamas

AWW, CUTE!

A type of humpless camel, llamas are famous for their droopy eyes, expressive ears, and sweet demeanor.

OH, YUCK!

There's nothing sweet about a startled llama. These woolly pack animals will launch gobs of spit at any animal they perceive as a threat—including humans!

Two-Toed Sloths

AWW, CUTE!

Perpetually good-natured and sluggish, sloths live their lives as if they're on permanent vacation. These tree-climbing natives of the South and Central American rain forests sleep 20 hours a day and spend their waking hours nibbling on fruit and leaves.

OH, YUCK!

Sloths in Peru have begun treating outdoor bathrooms like all-you-can-eat buffets. They climb into the cesspits beneath toilets and happily munch away on all the poop, pee, and even toilet paper!

5 ODD ANIMALS THAT PUT THE "WILD" IN WILDLIFE

TWO-HEADED TURTLE

THE BUSINESSMAN who bought this golden coin turtle in China got two heads for the price of one. Even better, the two heads seem to get along and will even share meals. Striking and rare, two-headed animals result when twins fail to separate before birth. The condition can strike many kinds of animals.

CYCLOPS SHARK

WHEN A FISHERMAN cut open the pregnant dusky shark he caught in the Gulf of California, he found something extra fishy: a baby shark with just one eye! Scientists studying the shark pup confirmed that it had cyclopedia, a rare birth defect that occurs in several species of animals, including humans. Baby cyclops sharks have been found in pregnant sharks before but never swimming freely in the ocean, which means you shouldn't fear any solo-eyed monsters circling you in the surf.

TWO-FACED KITTY

YOU MIGHT CALL any creature with three eyes, two mouths, and one brain a monster. The owner of this double-faced feline calls him Frank and Louie. Born with a rare disorder that duplicated the features on his furry head, Frank and Louie is one cat with two faces

RKS OF NATURE

(although he's blind in his middle eye and can only eat with his right mouth). Kittens born with this condition seldom survive, but 12-year-old Frank and Louie made the Guinness Book of World Records as the world's oldest two-faced cat.

DOUBLE-NOSED PIGLET

IT'S A SIGHT so freaky you might squeal with fright: a pig with two slobbery snouts and what appears to be a single eye. But this peculiar piglet, born on a farm in China, isn't some sort of porky cyclops. It actually has three eyes—one on either side of its snouts and a third in the middle. This little piggy was born with "polycephaly," a rare condition of having more than one head. The birth defect could end up saving this piglet's bacon; its owner has no intention of turning this special specimen into spiral ham.

WORLD'S UGLIEST DOG

A GATHERING FOR MUTTS with mugs that only their mothers could love, the annual "World's Ugliest Dog Contest" in Petaluma, California, celebrates canines that could pass muster as space monsters. The most famous champion was Sam, a Chinese crested hairless dog whose splotchy skin, soapy eyes, and wayward fangs clinched him the title for three years running. The pitiful pooch lived a happy life until he passed away in 2005, but the California contest continues to crown canines that could make children cry.

SURFACE

NOMURA'S JELLYFISH

This 400-pound (181.4 kg) sea monster has been invading the waters near Japan in record numbers. Fishermen are losing their catches to the jellyfish's toxic stingers, and one group even lost their boat! Their trawler capsized when the crew tried to haul in a net filled with dozens of these brainless, boneless blobs.

2,000 feet/
600 meters

GULPER EEL

With a mouth that hinges to consume fish and crab larger than its body, this jaw-dropping deep-sea monster can literally bite off more than it can chew. And because its teeth are too tiny to do much chewing, the eel deposits swallowed prey into a pelican-like pouch—a sort of gruesome waiting room for doomed fish awaiting digestion in the eel's stretchable stomach.

6,000 feet/
1,800 meters

FATHEAD SCULPIN

In all fairness to "Mr. Blobby" here (as he's been nicknamed by scientists), the fathead sculpin is not a fish that photographs well out of water. It's less repulsive in its deep-ocean habitat, where the crushing depths mold its flabby body into a more streamlined shape. Mr. Blobby is known to cruise the heated waters near volcanic vents.

4,000 feet/
1,200 meters

SEA MONSTERS!

Scientists know more about the surface of the moon than about the depths of the ocean, so it only makes sense that many deep-sea creatures look like space monsters! And the deeper you go, the grosser they get.

GIANT ISOPOD

A true monster from the deep, this 16-inch (41 cm) crustacean is actually a relative of the roly-poly pill bugs living in your backyard. When oil-rig workers in the Gulf of Mexico found one of these creepy crawlies clutching their submarine in 2010, they thought they'd discovered a sea monster!

7,020 feet / 2,140 meters

SUPERGIANT AMPHIPOD

As long as a football, these elusive scavengers feast on the flesh of dead fish and marine animals that fall into the ocean's deepest trenches. Scientists rarely find amphipods longer than an inch (2.5 cm). These "supergiant" versions were discovered in a deep-sea trench near New Zealand.

21,120 feet / 6,437 meters

OCEAN BOTTOM

PREPARE TO MEET THE KING AND QUEEN of ugly and mean in the animal kingdom. In this corner, soaking in a bucket of its own mucus, we have the hagfish, a primitive deep-sea creature with a nasty surprise for any predator desperate enough to take a bite. And in the other corner, the naked mole rat, a buck-toothed burrowing rodent that thinks it's a bug! Both of these awful animals embody everything that's nasty in nature, but only one can win the title of most gross. Let the battle begin!

GROSS GRUDGE MATCH

Naked Mole Rat

VS

APPEARANCE

NAKED MOLE RAT: Brownish pink and wrinkly like an overcooked hot dog, a naked mole rat has beady eyes, big incisor teeth, and a body that's nearly hairless—hence its "naked" name. The rat's loose skin helps it squeeze through the tight tunnels of its subterranean home. Nearly blind, the wrinkly rodent navigates using touch-sensitive whiskers. Hey, at least it's spared the horror of seeing other naked mole rats!

HAGFISH: As if the hagfish's eel-like body and tentacle-tipped mouth weren't ugly enough, this fish's skin is lined with glands that squirt sticky mucus. We're not talking just a quick spritz here—a hagfish can transform five gallons (19 liters) of seawater into slimy brine in minutes! Despite its abhorrent ability, the hagfish does have a lot of heart. Four of them, actually.

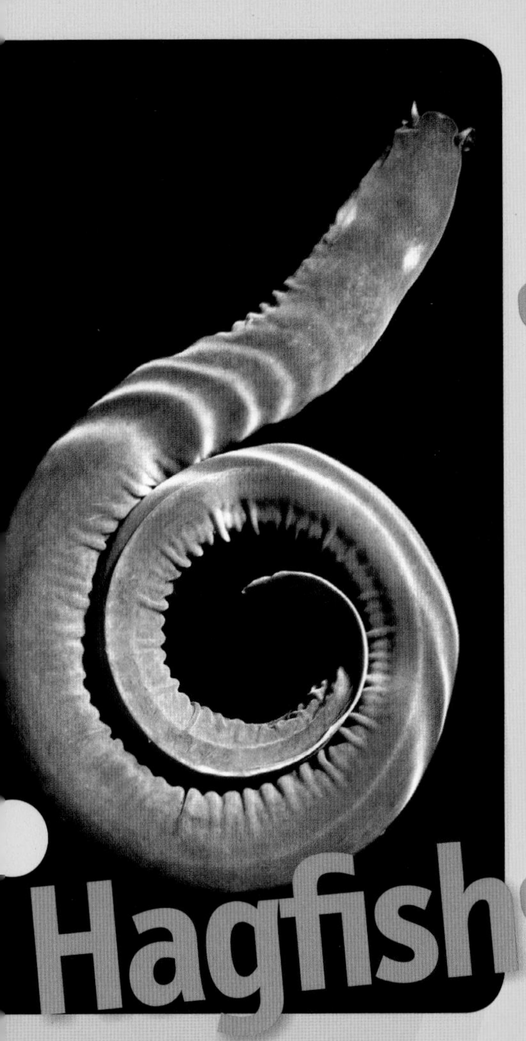

LIFESTYLE

NAKED MOLE RAT: The only mammals that live like insects, naked mole rats form close-knit colonies beneath the sun-baked grasslands of East Africa. Like ants, the rats take on the jobs of worker drones and soldiers, all charged with serving one very mean queen. This royal terror spends her days living large and bullying the other females. A chemical in the queen's pee prevents the other rats from reproducing and taking over her role as mama mole.

HAGFISH: Nearly blind and not very bright, hagfish bumble around the deep ocean looking for their next meal—while trying not to become something else's next meal! If a bigger fish starts trouble, it's slime time! The hagfish encases itself in a cocoon of protective mucus and emits enough extra goo to clog the predator's gills. If the slimed fish survives this suffocating coup de gross, it learns a valuable lesson: Never hassle a hagfish!

DIET

NAKED MOLE RAT: Tireless tunnellers, naked mole rats gnaw through the hard-packed earth in search of tasty roots and tubers, which they collect for the good of queen and colony. To supplement their meager diet, the workers snack on their own poop—and even share it with others. See, not all naked mole rats are as mean as their queen!

HAGFISH: Rotting fish smells like Thanksgiving dinner to the sensitive sense organs of a hagfish. With its hornlike mouthparts and rasping tongue, this slimy monster burrows into the bodies of dead or ailing sea creatures and eats them from the inside out.

SPECIAL ABILITIES

NAKED MOLE RAT: Roughly one-fourth of a naked mole rat's muscle mass is located in its jaws, giving the critter incredible biting power. It can even chew through concrete!

HAGFISH: In danger of choking on their own slime, hagfish have learned an amazing trick to rid their bodies of ooze. They tie themselves in knots and wring out the slime from head to tail.

THE HAGFISH!

Even if you were to dress a naked mole rat in a dapper suit and tie, it would still be one ugly rodent. Nevertheless, the sickening powers of slime will win out every time. We're just glad both of these animals rarely see the light of day.

Little Red Flying Fox

Not all bats are creepy. Climb up close to a flying fox—a type of tree-dwelling fruit bat—and you'll swear you're eye-to-eye with a winged puppy dog!

Seen from the right angle, these creepy creatures are practically cute!

DiSGUSTiNGLY *Adorable*

Red-Lipped Batfish

This pouty-lipped fish uses its lower fins to walk awkwardly across the seafloor rather than swim.

Aye-Aye

Found only on the island of Madagascar, this itty-bitty relative of chimps, apes, and humans uses its extra-long middle finger to dig bugs from tree branches.

Cuttlefish

A master of morphing, this mollusk can change the color and even the texture of its skin to hide from predators or hypnotize prey. It can go from cute to ugly to invisible in less than a second!

Jumping Spider

A fearsome hunter, the jumping spider spots prey with its powerful peepers—including a pair on the back of its head—before pouncing up to 50 times the length of its body.

HEAVY HEART

The heart of a blue whale can weigh up to a ton (907 kg)—as much as a **COMPACT CAR.**

COW SLICKS

To help digest its grassy diet, a typical cow makes more than **13 GALLONS** (49 liters) of saliva every day!

FAT SCAT

Seven hours is all it takes for an **AFRICAN ELEPHANT** to produce enough poop to outweigh a full-grown human.

Creepy CREATURE CALCULATIONS

GAG GAUGE

UGLY ANiMALS

Daryl the Dung Beetle Ranks **NATURE'S NASTIES**

CHAPTER 4

Creepy Crawlies

WITHOUT BUGS, SLUGS, SNAILS, AND worms, we'd all be in deep doo-doo. Literally! Many of these creepy creepers feast on feces and dead plant matter, making Earth a cleaner planet in the process. You should thank them for doing their disgusting job, but that doesn't mean you'd invite a deathstalker scorpion to dinner—or allow a leech to suck your blood for its dinner! Prepare to squirm as we explore the wriggling world of multi-legged monsters, tongue-eating parasites, and ... zombie bugs?

ATTACK OF THE ARTHROPODS!

WE SWAT THEM, WE SQUISH THEM—we even dip them in drawn butter and eat them—but we'll never overthrow the arthropods. The real rulers of the creature kingdom, arthropods include flies, beetles, spiders, mites, lobsters, shrimp, scorpions, and centipedes. If it has at least six legs, a segmented body, and wears its skeleton like a suit of armor, it's an arthropod!

More than 80 percent of all species belong to this wildly diverse animal phylum, and biologists are discovering new bugs all the time. Arthropods buzz above the trees, creep underground, and scurry through the darkest depths of the ocean. You probably have some clinging to your body right now. Feeling itchy yet?

Despite a few exceptions—that charming ladybug on your windowsill or the radiant butterfly flitting through your garden—arthropods are the all-stars of nastiness. They bite. They sting. They spread disease. They guzzle our blood and can plant their babies in our bodies. Their furry legs and fearsome fangs inspire sweat-inducing phobias. Put simply: **ARTHROPODS BUG US.**

ARTHROPOD SQUADS

Whether they buzz, swim, or scurry, most bugs belong to one of these three main groups ...

INSECTS

CHARACTERISTICS: Six legs and three body segments

SAMPLE SPECIES: Ants, bees, cockroaches, grasshoppers, and butterflies

SPECIAL ABILITIES: Insects are the only arthropods that can fly. Some dragonflies can zoom up to 30 mph (48 kph)!

MVP (MOST VULGAR PLAYER): Bombardier beetle—This breed of beetle packs heat! A bombardier can squirt a boiling cocktail of chemicals from the business end of its abdomen. The spray melts attacking insects and sears human skin.

ARACHNIDS

CHARACTERISTICS: Eight legs and two body segments

SAMPLE SPECIES: Spiders, ticks, mites, and scorpions

SPECIAL ABILITIES: Spiders can spin webs of superstrong silk to snare prey. They instill greater fear in humans than any other animal, despite the fact that spiders are relatively harmless compared to insects.

MVP (MOST VULGAR PLAYER): Chigger—While still in its larval stage, this microscopic mite seeks a warm-blooded body—you, for instance—and injects it with flesh-melting saliva. Chiggers slurp up the digested tissue of their hosts, leaving behind itchy welts.

CRUSTACEANS

CHARACTERISTICS: Ten or more legs. Most live in lakes, rivers, and oceans.

SAMPLE SPECIES: Crabs, lobsters, shrimp, crayfish, and barnacles

SPECIAL ABILITIES: Crustaceans have short swimming legs called swimmerets. You probably consider them the tastiest of the arthropods. Large crustaceans such as Alaskan king crab and Maine lobster sell for more than 12 bucks a pound (.45 kg) in seafood restaurants.

MVP (MOST VULGAR PLAYER): Sacculina—Like some alien from a monster movie, this freeloading barnacle grabs any passing crab and implants it with a tiny sluglike creature. The slug sprouts tendrils that wrap around the crab's body and eventually force it to raise the slug's larvae, which squirt into the ocean and continue the disgusting cycle.

DARYL THE DUNG BEETLE'S FOUL FACTS

Powerful gas-passers, wood-munching termites produce an explosive amount of flatulence for their size. Some scientists believe they contribute to global warming!

Buggy Behavior

Nasty Habits of Successful Arthropods

Wolf Spider

THEY PRODUCE LIKE CRAZY!

Pest control is a billion-dollar business for a reason: Bugs are really good at making other bugs. A single female aphid, for example, can produce 600 billion offspring in one season! **WOLF SPIDERS** lay dozens of eggs several times a year. The squirming hatchlings hitchhike on their mama's back for protection. Why the population explosion? It's a bug-eat-bug world out there, and a big family ensures survival.

THEY VOMIT ON YOUR FOOD!

Keep an eye on that **HOUSEFLY** hovering over the dinner table. Chances are it already upchucked on your French fries and tossed its cookies over your apple pie. Lacking teeth of any type, flies vomit digestive juices on everything they eat and then slurp it up like a sickening soup. As if that wasn't nasty enough, flies taste your food first with little hairs on their feet!

THEY SHED THEIR SKELETONS!

Imagine peeling off your skin and leaving it in a fleshy pile on the floor. Arthropods change their shells, made from a natural armor called chitin, just like we change our clothes. When a bug grows too big for its chitinous britches, it sheds the old skeleton—a revolting process called molting—and grows a new one. The old armor is left behind, although giant centipedes will actually eat their discarded skeletons. Nasty, right? At least you can't call them litter bugs!

THEY FREELOAD!

Many arthropods are parasites, meaning they survive inside a living host. These life-sucking relationships are often the stuff of nightmares. Take, for instance, the **TONGUE-EATING LOUSE.** This small crustacean enters the body of an unsuspecting fish through its gills. Once it reaches the fish's mouth, the louse devours the tongue—then takes its place to feed off the fish's blood and mucus! Fortunately, the fish doesn't seem to notice that its tongue is now a monster.

THEY MAKE ZOMBIE BUGS!

The **FEMALE JEWEL WASP** is a master of mind control. It seeks out a cockroach and injects its brain with venom, which turns the roach into a zombified drone that mindlessly follows the wasp to her burrow. There, she lays her egg on the roach's shell. Stupefied but alive, the poor cockroach spends its final days as food for the wasp's larva.

Meanwhile, in South America, the **FEMALE PHORID FLY** makes fire ants miserable by injecting them with her eggs. Each newly hatched fly munches on its host's brain, compelling the ant to march far from its colony so that other fire ants won't attack it. Eventually, the baby fly decapitates the ant and hatches from its head.

KILLING CAPACITY

LOW → HIGH

ASIAN GIANT HORNET

WHERE IT LIVES: Asia, particularly Japan

STINGING SENSATION: A bulbous bug with a body the size of your thumb and wings that could span your hand. Its quarter-inch (6 mm) stinger injects venom that dissolves flesh and feels like a hot nail. Honeybees have the most to fear from these oversized insects. Just a few Asian giant hornets can tear through 10,000 bees, leaving behind nothing but bit-off heads and legs. About 40 people die each year from allergic reactions to this hornet's sting.

DEATHSTALKER SCORPION

WHERE IT LIVES: The deserts of North Africa and the Middle East

DESERT MENACE: With their glistening shells, furry claws, and stinger-tipped tails, scorpions might look like lethal little monsters, but most aren't deadly. The deathstalker is one scary exception. Its potent venom can kill babies and old people, although healthy kids and adults typically survive the agonizing sting. Believe it or not, some people keep deathstalkers as pets!

AFRICANIZED BEE

WHERE IT LIVES: From South America to the southeastern United States

PERFECT SWARM: The product of a beekeeping experiment gone awry, this highly aggressive breed of honeybee escaped from Brazil in 1957 and has been heading north ever since. Dubbed "killer bees" by the media, they'll pursue any threat until it drops—and then continue stinging and stinging and stinging! A swarm chasing a Texas man pierced him with more than a thousand stings!

SYDNEY FUNNEL-WEB SPIDER

WHERE IT LIVES: In and around Sydney, Australia

BITTER BITER: A big spider with a bad attitude, this Australian native attacks anything that provokes it, rearing up on furry legs to brandish fangs dripping with venom. Once riled up, the funnel-web spider will bite and bite and bite some more. Victims could croak in an hour if they don't receive the widely available antivenom.

MOSQUITO

WHERE IT LIVES: Tropical and mild climates around the world

DISEASE SPREADER: Next time you smack a mosquito that's slurping blood from your skin, consider this: You were just bitten by the world's deadliest animal! Millions of people perish each year from mosquito bites in Africa and elsewhere. These buzzing, bothersome flies spread malaria, dengue fever, and other diseases that are fatal if left untreated.

Killer Bugs

The 5 Deadliest Creepy Crawlies

Stay far away from these nasty insects and arachnids, listed in order of lethality.

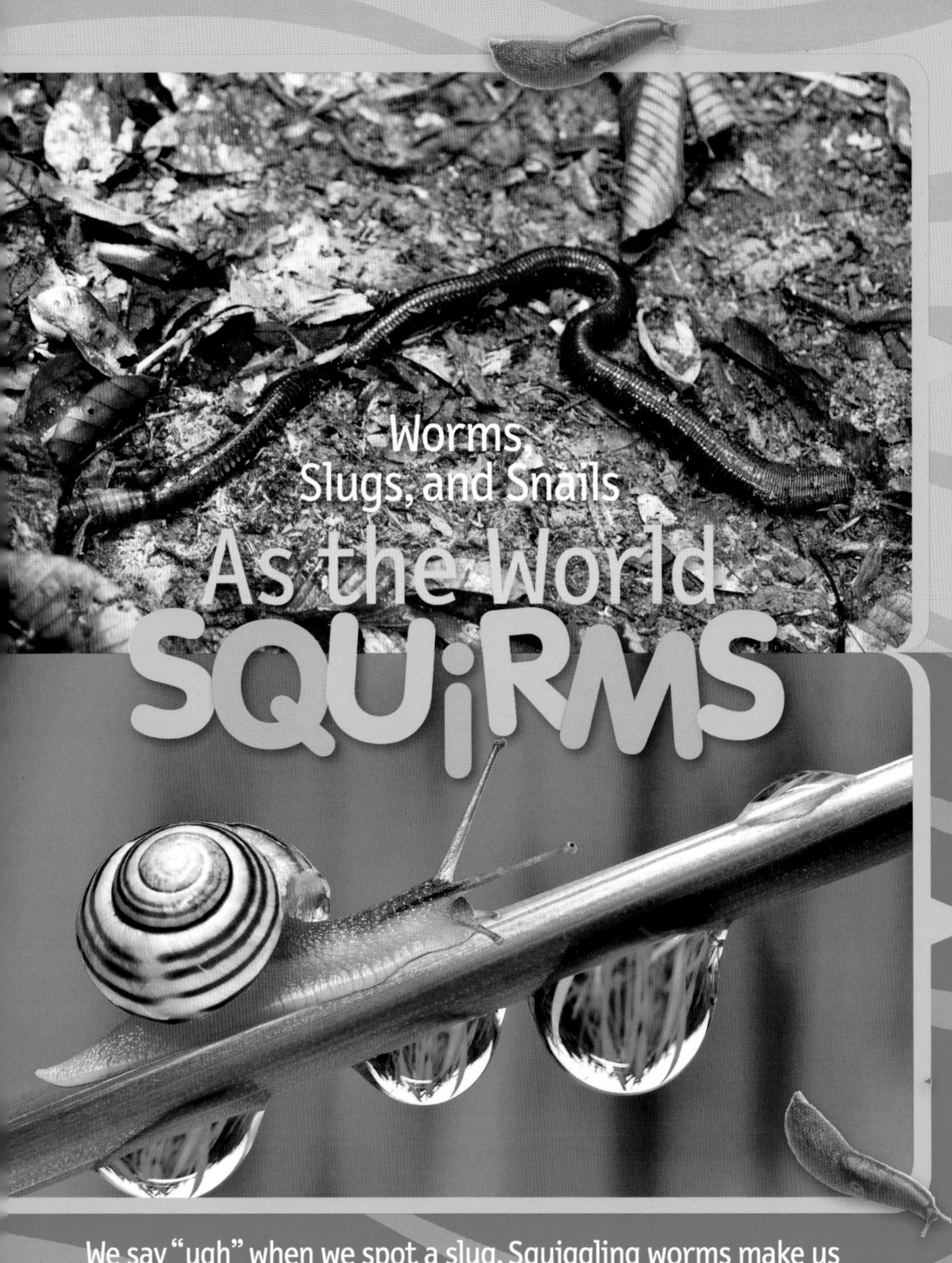

Worms, Slugs, and Snails
As the World SQUIRMS

We say "ugh" when we spot a slug. Squiggling worms make us woozy. Snails leave trails that leave us feeling unwell. Why all the revulsion? After all, earthworms rarely squirm in plain sight, and even a sloth could outrun a slug. To understand the source of our unease, let's unearth all the dirt on these slimy trailblazers.

WORMS!

"Worm" is an all-purpose term used to describe just about any squiggling noodle-like animal that lacks arms, legs, and a backbone. Biologists classify them by body type. Segmented "annelids" include earthworms and bloodsucking leeches. "Flatworms" have squashed bodies and beady eyes. "Nematodes" are round and smooth to the touch. Worms live on land, in the water, and sometimes inside other living creatures—including humans!

THE GOOD: Dirt-dwelling worms are part of nature's cleanup crew. Earthworms devour decomposing animals, decaying plants, and fecal matter while excreting nutrient-rich poop that supercharges the soil for seedlings. They do this dirty job everywhere except Antarctica.

THE BAD: Many types of worms—particularly roundworms and flatworms—are parasites, which means...

THE YUCKY: One particularly icky parasite is the Guinea worm, a skinny nematode that people pick up by drinking contaminated water. The worm spends a year growing inside its host's intestines, eventually reaching up to 3 feet (1 meter) in length. Once it runs out of room to roam, the Guinea worm makes a painful exit in its host's leg. The victim must slowly tug the worm from his or her body while wrapping it around a stick like a never-ending spaghetti noodle.

SNAILS & SLUGS!

Ever wondered what a snail looks like naked but were too polite to peek under its shell? Look at a slug! It's the same slimy animal—creepy eyestalks and all—except without the protective casing. Both snails and slugs are gastropods, which is Latin for "stomach-foot." Finding a snail or slug is simple: Just follow its slime trail. Made of snotty mucus, this foul-tasting goop protects the animal from predators. It also makes its muscular foot slippery for faster movement across the forest floor. Not that you'd notice. It took a snail two minutes to travel 13 inches (33 cm) at the annual World Snail Racing Championships in Norfolk, England—and that was the world champion!

THE GOOD: Like worms, snails and slugs are the ultimate recyclers. They munch on dead organic matter and turn it into fertilizer. Snails are also a rich source of protein for people all over the world. Fancy restaurants serve escargot (pronounced "ess-cargo"), a savory dish of cooked snails.

THE BAD: Snails and slugs devour living plants as well as decaying matter, making them a headache for gardeners and farmers. Some carnivorous sea snails can deliver a lethal sting.

THE YUCKY: Snail eyestalks are icky enough. Eyestalks infected with *Leucochloridium paradoxum*, a type of parasitic flatworm, are downright freaky! The worm fills the eyestalks from the inside with its larvae, which pulsate and flash in hypnotic patterns. Hungry birds see the snail's wriggling eyestalks and think they're caterpillars. Any birds that eat the stalks become the worm's next unfortunate host. The snail's icky-eyed nightmare, meanwhile, begins from scratch. It grows a new pair of larvae-filled eyestalks and must suffer through another aerial assault.

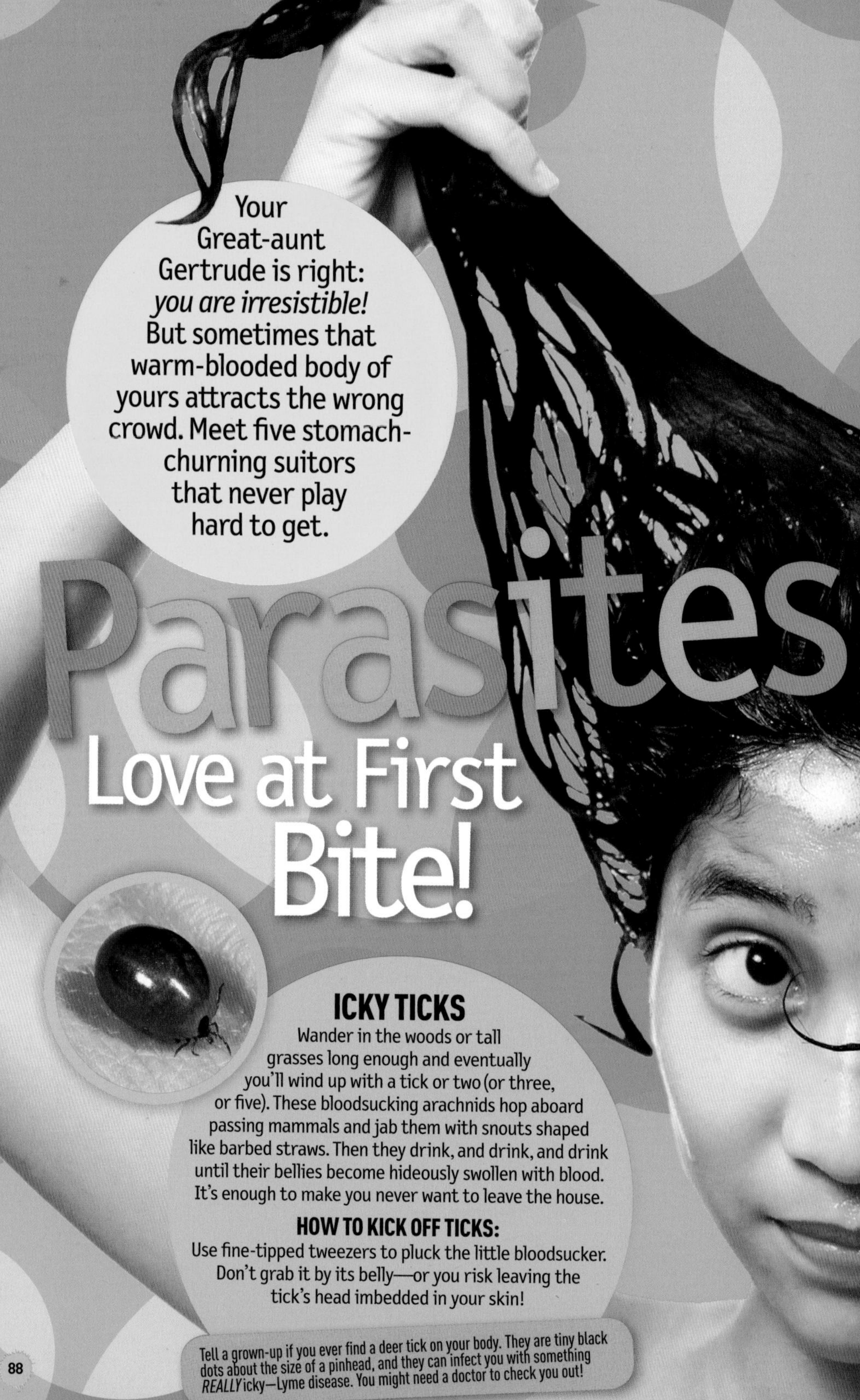

Your Great-aunt Gertrude is right: *you are irresistible!* But sometimes that warm-blooded body of yours attracts the wrong crowd. Meet five stomach-churning suitors that never play hard to get.

Parasites

Love at First Bite!

ICKY TICKS

Wander in the woods or tall grasses long enough and eventually you'll wind up with a tick or two (or three, or five). These bloodsucking arachnids hop aboard passing mammals and jab them with snouts shaped like barbed straws. Then they drink, and drink, and drink until their bellies become hideously swollen with blood. It's enough to make you never want to leave the house.

HOW TO KICK OFF TICKS:

Use fine-tipped tweezers to pluck the little bloodsucker. Don't grab it by its belly—or you risk leaving the tick's head imbedded in your skin!

Tell a grown-up if you ever find a deer tick on your body. They are tiny black dots about the size of a pinhead, and they can infect you with something *REALLY* icky—Lyme disease. You might need a doctor to check you out!

LOUSY LICE

Itty-bitty insects with claw-tipped legs, head lice latch to your hair and slurp blood from your scalp, inflicting a maddening itch. A female louse lays eggs called nits—around five a day—which she carefully sticks to each hair shaft. (Now you can tell your friends where the term "nit-picking" comes from!) Lice spread through body contact or the sharing of headwear. Anything infested with lice is called "lousy." Seriously!

HOW TO LOSE LICE:
Pick their nits, lather with smelly shampoo, or shave your head.

SCARY SCABIES

The aptly named "itch mite" really knows how to get under your skin. This eight-legged parasite burrows into your flesh, causing itchy red welts that simply must ... be ... scratched—a condition called scabies. Itch mites treat your body like a suburb, laying eggs and raising larvae that mature and move just down the block—perhaps the inside of your elbow or the next knuckle over. You can catch scabies from close contact with anyone who has it, although it's not nearly as contagious as head lice.

HOW TO SAY SEE YA TO SCABIES:
Apply mite-killing ointments.

ABHORRENT BOTFLIES

Most insects will make your skin crawl, but the human botfly actually makes it wriggle! These fat-bodied flies plant their eggs on mosquitoes, which drop off their cargo when they bite humans. The eggs hatch under your skin and unleash writhing white larvae that take weeks to mature.

HOW TO BEAT BOTFLIES:
Botfly removal is best left to doctors, who wield the tools and antiseptics needed to slice these horrible hitchhikers safely from your skin.

TERRIFYING TAPEWORMS

Meet the world's worst dinner guest! This nasty nematode infiltrates your body through undercooked meat and makes its home in your intestines, where it helps itself to everything you eat. A tapeworm can swipe your body's nutrients for years and grow to a length of 12 feet (4 meters)! Most hosts don't realize they're infected until they spot tapeworm bits in their poop.

HOW TO TERMINATE TAPEWORMS:
Take some tapeworm-killing medicine.

TITAN BEETLE

You wouldn't want to pick up this beast of a beetle for two reasons: It's larger than your hand, and its fanglike mandibles are strong enough to snap a pencil. Adult titan beetles spend their days flying through the forest on the hunt for mates. Stricken with lovesickness, they don't even bother eating!

THE AMAZON JUNGLE

Freaky FOREST

WELCOME TO THE WORLD'S WORST PICNIC SPOT: South America's Amazon rain forest. It is home to a tenth of all known animal species, most of which are insects and arachnids—including some of the largest on Earth! Entomologists (or bug scientists) are in heaven here; everyone else should watch their step.

AMAZONIAN GIANT CENTIPEDE

Forty-three claw-tipped legs propel this voracious foot-long (30.5 cm) predator in pursuit of lizards, mice, frogs, and even bats. Pity the centipede's prey, which it pins to the ground with powerful pincers that inject a poison potent enough to make humans sick.

ARMY ANT

It's the world's deadliest parade: a million army ants, marching blindly across the forest floor like a carnivorous moving carpet. Wielding massive mandibles, the ants shred any creatures too sluggish to get out of their way. The lesson of this story: Never take a nap in the Amazon rain forest.

GOLIATH BIRD-EATING SPIDER

This relative of the tarantula grows to the size of a catcher's mitt and sprouts inch-long (2.5 cm) fangs. The goliath feeds on birds, rodents, and insects that wander into its burrow. Humans have little to fear from the spider's mild bite, although spiny hairs launched from the goliath's abdomen can irritate the skin.

T. REX LEECH

It's not the largest leech in the rain forest (that would be the giant Amazonian leech, which grows as long as your arm) but the *Tyrannobdella rex* is the most disturbing. While other leeches drink blood, the awesomely named *T. rex* has a taste for mucous membranes. Swimmers in the Amazon have left the river with these "tyrant leech kings" latched inside their noses.

Whip Spider

Like an arachnid version of Indiana Jones, this leggy spider lashes out with its whiplike forelegs to snare prey.

These ugly insects promise not to bite—HONEST!

HiDEOUS BUT Harmless

Giant African Millipede

Lacking the venomous bite of a giant centipede, this 10-inch (25 cm) monster is actually a popular pet!

Mole Cricket

With an odd body built for burrowing, swimming, and flight, the off-putting mole cricket is an all-terrain terror.

Giant Burrowing Cockroach

This heavyweight champ of the cockroach family also goes by the bold name "rhinoceros cockroach."

Giant Weta

Fear not this fist-size insect! Not only would it rather skitter away than bite you, the giant weta lives only on a small island off New Zealand's coast.

LOTTA LEGS

Nearly 10,000 bugs might live in just **ONE SQUARE FOOT (930 SQ CM)** of forest floor.

WEB WARY

Eighteen percent of men and 55 percent of women suffer from arachnophobia: **THE FEAR OF SPIDERS.**

SKEETER FEEDERS

Twenty percent of people are **MORE ATTRACTIVE** to mosquitoes, and thus bitten more often.

Buggy INFO

GAG GAUGE

CREEPY CRAWLiES

Daryl the Dung Beetle Ranks **UGLY BUGS**

BLAAARGH!

Deathstalker Scorpion

Whip Spider

SICKENING

Giant Centipede

Asian Giant Hornet

UNSETTLING

Sydney Funnel-Web Spider

CHAPTER 5

Gross Across the Globe

STINKY SEWAGE, FEARSOME FLATULENCE, MAGGOTY GARBAGE,

squiggling tentacles—some things are disgusting no matter where you hang your hat. Well, unless you happen to live in Japan, where live octopus is a delicacy. Oh, or in France, where tooting has a lighthearted history. (French bakers whip up a tasty pastry called Pets de Nonne, which basically means a nun passing gas.) And before you wrinkle your nose at a bowl of rotten Alaskan fish heads, wait until you find out what's in your hot dog! What you consider nasty, someone across the world might think is nice, or sacred, or downright delicious!

Disturbing DESTINATIONS

BUBBLEGUM ALLEY

THE PLACE: San Luis Obispo, California
Stringy gobs of chewed gum plaster the walls on both sides of this 70-foot-long alley (21 m). Locals and tourists have been "decorating" this sticky spot for decades.

ISLAND OF DOLLS

THE PLACE: Xochimilco, Mexico
Battered, mold-spattered dolls hang from tree branches on this creepy peninsula near Mexico City.

THE BLARNEY STONE

THE PLACE: Cork, Ireland

This stone built into Blarney Castle is supposed to impart powers of poetic speech upon those who kiss it, but would you want to plant your lips on something that's been smooched by thousands of tourists every month? Blech!

PLASTINARIUM

THE PLACE: Guben, Germany

See the preserved-in-plastic bodies of humans and animals from the inside out, sliced neatly into cross sections or poised for action at this astounding anatomical museum.

MÜTTER MUSEUM

THE PLACE: Philadelphia, Pennsylvania

Meander through two floors of medical monstrosities—from an oversized human colon to a display of animal brains—at this museum originally opened to train physicians.

THE PLACE: Deshnok, India
Oh, rats! Thousands of the furry rodents scamper through this ornate Hindu temple, where they are considered sacred. Tourists leave their shoes at the door and wander barefoot. It's considered good luck if a rat touches your toes!

KARNI MATA TEMPLE

PART TWO: EASTERN HEMISPHERE

Disturbing DESTINATIONS

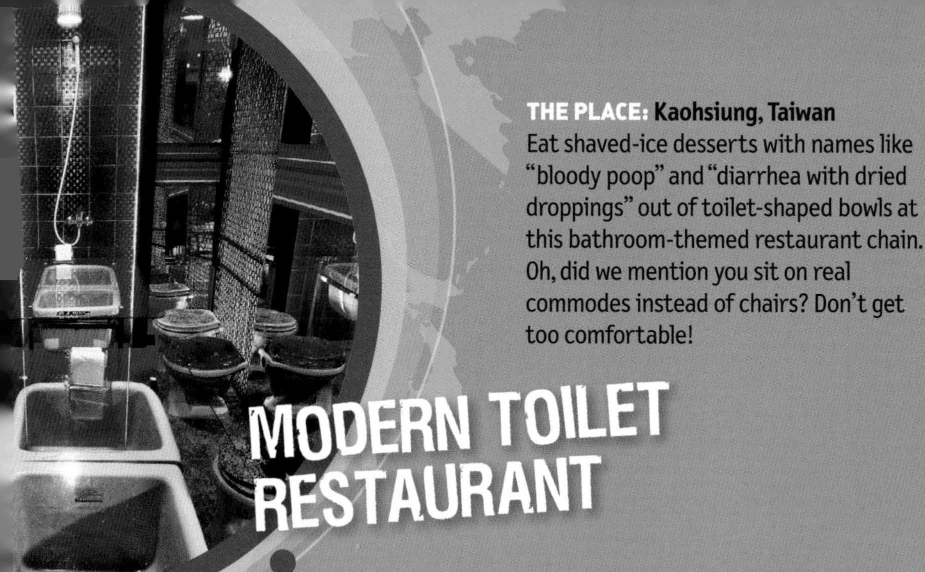

THE PLACE: **Kaohsiung, Taiwan**
Eat shaved-ice desserts with names like "bloody poop" and "diarrhea with dried droppings" out of toilet-shaped bowls at this bathroom-themed restaurant chain. Oh, did we mention you sit on real commodes instead of chairs? Don't get too comfortable!

MODERN TOILET RESTAURANT

THE PLACE: **Waitomo, New Zealand**
They may look like constellations of pretty blue stars to the visitors who explore these perpetually dark caverns by boat, but the lights that dot the ceiling are actually glow-in-the-dark bug lures created by fly larvae to snare insects in sticky strands of mucus.

GLOWWORM CAVES

THE PLACE: **Territory of Christmas Island, Australia**
If the crab tank at your local seafood restaurant makes you queasy, steer clear of this tiny island during the fall months, when millions of red crab scurry over every inch of ground as they migrate to the ocean.

CRAB ISLAND

Bracken BAT CAVE

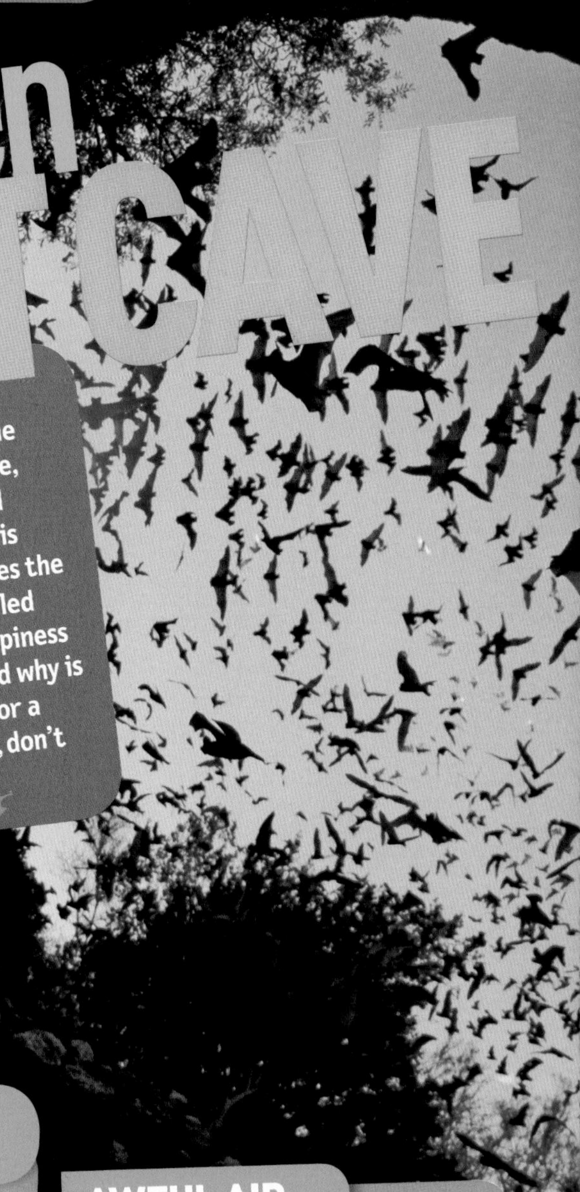

BATS AND BUGS might call it home sweet home, but to everyone else, Texas' Bracken Cave is the Grand Central Station of grossness. This subterranean chamber combines the toxic atmosphere of a roach-filled sewer with the perpetual creepiness of a bat-crammed cave. Oh, and why is the ground moving? Suit up for a peek inside. Whatever you do, don't dawdle!

THE SKY IS POOPING!

THE SKY IS POOPING!

The cave's bats swarm from the cave's mouth every night to feast on 125 tons (113 MT) of tasty insects. All those crunchy bugs make for a lot of bat pee and feces—called "guano"—which falls to the cave floor in a repulsive rain all summer long. Soon, thick sand consisting of bat poop is knee-high in the cave.

AWFUL AIR

Entering Bracken Cave is a bad idea, but lingering too long could be suicide! The bat poop oozes a fog of toxic ammonia. Workers who mine the guano for fertilizer have to wear gas masks or they'll get sick. Gosh, is guano really that valuable?

GOING BATTY

You think one bat is creepy? Try hanging with 20 million of them! Each spring, Mexican free-tailed bats migrate from south of the U.S. border to raise their pups in Bracken Cave. Sticky bodily fluids drip from above as the bats have babies. Up to 500 pups can crowd into one square foot (929 sq cm) of ceiling space!

EAGER EATERS

Take a closer look at the guano-caked cave floor and you'll see that it seethes with wriggling insects. Excrement-eating bugs keep the poop from piling too high, while flesh-devouring beetles make fast food of any unfortunate bats that plummet to the floor while learning to fly. Picked clean of meat in mere minutes, bat skeletons are everywhere. You would suffer the same fate if you got stuck here!

DARYL THE DUNG BEETLE'S FOUL FACTS

DEER CAVE IN BORNEO is home to a mountain of guano more than **300 FEET** (91 meters) high. Hey, I think I just found my next vacation spot!

FOND OF FLINGING YOUR FOOD?

Then fly to the Spanish town of Buñol in August, where 40,000 people chuck overripe tomatoes at each other during the festival of La Tomatina, the world's biggest food fight. Or you can zip to Scotland and take part in a pre-wedding ritual called "blackening of the bride and groom." Friends of the betrothed soak them with rotten eggs and sticky sauces. After all, if the couple can survive that disgusting barrage, married life should be a piece of cake!

GROSS Getaways

Good Places for BAD HABITS

THINK FECES IS FUNNY?

Then spend your holidays in Catalonia, Spain. Here, for the last two centuries, residents have been spicing up their nativity scenes with a peculiar figurine known as the caganer. The little guy takes many forms—peasants, sports stars, heads of state—but he always strikes a squatting pose and bears a little brown lump beneath his bare bottom. Holiday revelers are encouraged to find "the pooper" in each nativity scene. It's like a dookie-themed take on *Where's Waldo*!

BIG ON BURPING?

Then make tracks for Singapore, where diners display their post-meal satisfaction with a *gentle* burp. The emphasis is on gentle here. Rattling the rafters with a monster belch is unacceptable in any culture.

LOVE SLURPING YOUR NOODLES?

Then visit Japan, where the locals proudly eat their ramen loudly. The proper way to ingest each skinny strand is to suck it up with an intake of cool air (which also protects your tongue from broth burns). Eating ramen too quietly is a sign that you're not enjoying it, so think of each slobbery slurp as a compliment to the chef!

FANCY DIVING INTO A DUMPSTER?

Then head to New York City, a major hub for "freeganism." This social movement is about making the most of the world's limited resources, but accomplishing this noble motive involves some extreme recycling. Rather than spend money at the store, freegans, as they're called, grab all their goods, including any food that hasn't gone bad, straight from the garbage.

Sloppy SEAS

We Set a Course for the EASTERN PACIFIC GARBAGE PATCH

SIGNS OF LAND ARE EVERYWHERE, even a thousand miles (1,600 km) from shore, in the vast expanse of the Pacific Ocean midway between Hawaii and California. Bleach bottles and old garbage bins bob amid fishing nets tangled with rotting sea creatures. Twine, toothbrushes, discarded toys, to-go bags, and less identifiable pieces of plastic drift around and around in an enormous ocean vortex created by currents, sort of like a slowly flushing toilet that never drains. Scientists call this swirling mass of trash the Eastern Pacific Garbage Patch. Twice the size of Texas by some estimates, it's the world's largest dump. Don't let its name mislead you: The garbage patch isn't an island of trash. But the reality of its toxic composition is even more disturbing than its scattered mess of detergent bottles and fishing debris. Much of the patch is actually a sort of plastic soup!

Roughly 260 million tons (236 million MT) of plastic are produced each year worldwide, and as much as 10 percent of it ends up in the ocean. Soda bottles tumble into the surf. Garbage cans fall off ships. Grocery bags blow out to sea. Unlike food and other organic garbage, plastic doesn't dissolve; it just breaks into smaller and smaller pieces that can stick around for centuries.

Sea turtles, fish, and marine mammals choke on the larger pieces. Scientists fear that the plastic will block sunlight from reaching plankton, the tiny organisms that form the basis of the ocean's food chain. If plankton populations nosedive, the entire marine ecosystem will suffer.

Unfortunately, the Eastern Pacific Garbage Patch isn't unique. Similar trash vortexes swirl near Japan and in the North Atlantic. Skimming all the microplastics from these patches is an impossible mission, but it's never too late to cut down on our use of plastic. Otherwise, a day at the beach might turn into a sickening swim in plastic soup.

What's for Dinner?

UNUSUAL FOODS FROM AROUND THE WORLD

You might think these exotic dishes sound toxic, but they're actually delicacies in their home countries. As your mom might say, don't knock 'em, till you try 'em!

BIRD'S NEST SOUP

WHERE IT'S SERVED: China
For centuries, brave hunters have climbed the walls of bat-infested caves in Southeast Asia to gather the delicate nests of a small bird called a swift. Made of the swift's saliva, the nests are boiled for hours until they become a flavorless goo that's added to chicken broth and served for as much as 60 bucks a bowl. Pretty pricey for bird spit!

DURIAN

WHERE IT'S SERVED: Indonesia
Known wherever it's eaten as the "king of fruits," the dangerous-looking durian is notorious for raising such a royal stink—resembling a mix of sewage, vomit, and gym socks—that's it's often outlawed indoors. Its taste has been described as a mixture of cream cheese, almond-flavored custard, and rotten onions. Here's hoping durian fans follow the fruit with a breath mint.

SLÁTUR

WHERE IT'S SERVED: Iceland
After Icelandic ranchers slaughter their sheep every autumn, they serve slátur, a bloody mix of the animals' leftover bits (typically kidneys and livers) sewn into a sheep's stomach. The Scottish devour a similarly sickening recipe called haggis. Another version of slátur mixes lamb's blood and spices into sausage casings—a dish aptly named "blood pudding" elsewhere.

HOT DOGS

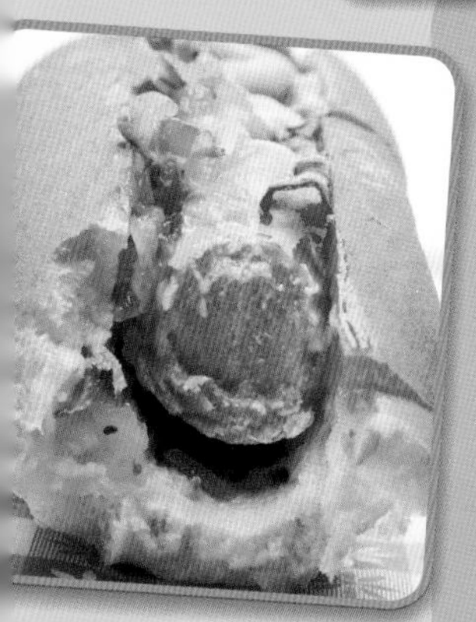

WHERE IT'S SERVED: United States
What could possibly be gross about America's favorite meat treat? The nastiness is right on the ingredients label. Sodium erythorbate for maintaining the meat's pink color. Potassium lactate for killing bacteria. A filler called maltodextrin. "Flavorings." Yes, hot dogs do contain pork, but along with it comes "any amount" of mechanically separated poultry, a pastelike substance defined as "a poultry product produced by forcing bones, with attached edible tissue, through a sieve or similar device under high pressure to separate bone from the edible tissue." Pass the relish!

CASU MARZU

WHERE IT'S SERVED: Italy
Uh-oh! This cheese is infested with maggots! Time to toss it in the trash, right? Wrong. In the Sardinian region of Italy, food lovers treasure this rancid rind, which is deliberately left outdoors for flies to fill with their eggs. The result is a cheesy mass of maggot poop best eaten while wearing safety glasses. After all, nothing kills the appetite like having a maggot leap into your eye!

LIVE SNAKE HEART

WHERE IT'S SERVED: Vietnam, Thailand
The two-step recipe for this Southeast Asian dish is as simple as it is gruesome. Step one: Slice a cobra open lengthwise along its entire body. Step two: Swallow the snake's heart *while it's still beating*! Those who've partaken of this heart-stopping hors d'oeuvre claim they can feel the snake's ticker still pumping as it slides down their throats.

DARYL THE DUNG BEETLE'S FOUL FACTS

LUWAK COFFEE—a type of Indonesian java brewed from beans that were eaten and excreted by a catlike mammal called a palm civet—sells for **$160 A POUND!** Worth every penny, if you ask me.

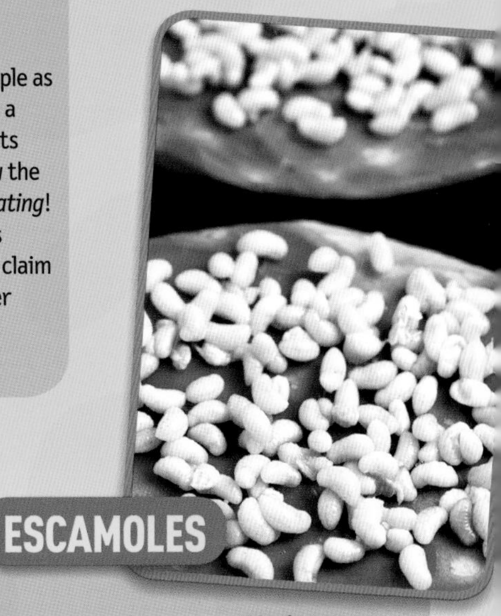

ESCAMOLES

WHERE IT'S SERVED: Mexico
Also known as "insect caviar," escamoles are the larval form of black ants, which are boiled until they reach the consistency of cottage cheese. They're just one of many, many, *many* insect dishes popular around the world. Turn the page for a sample of this bug buffet!

A Five-Course Feast of International Insect Dishes

Bug Appétit

IMAGINE FINDING A BUG IN YOUR SOUP—and asking for seconds! In many parts of the world, insects are just another food group. And why not? Bugs are rich in protein and vitamins. They take fewer resources to raise than cows, pigs, and chickens (all of which can spread illnesses if improperly raised or processed). Unlike bottom-feeding shrimp, which we pop in our mouths without a second thought, many bugs live on a wholesome diet of grass, leaves, and flowers. They also have a taste for farmers' crops, so eating invasive insects helps protect our veggies. Win-win!

Still, the idea of turning grubs into grub might squash your squeamish appetite, so we've described the taste of every buggy dish in this five-course meal gathered from across the globe.

APPETIZER: MOPANI WORM

Where it's eaten: Africa
How it's prepared: Squash this caterpillar to squirt out its green guts, then boil its body in salt water. Leave the boiled bug outside to dry in the sun.
What's it taste like? Eaten dried as a finger food, the chewy mopani worm tastes salty—a bit like beef jerky. Rehydrated and served in stew, it adds an earthy dash of wild-mushroom flavor.

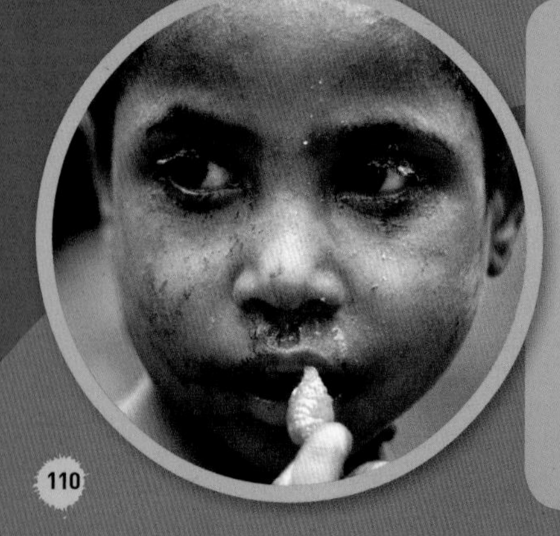

SOUP COURSE: SAGO GRUB

Where it's eaten: New Guinea, Thailand, Central America, Asia, and Africa
How it's prepared: Plucked from the inside of palm trees, this larval form of the palm weevil is often rolled in a hot pan with no other ingredients. It's a popular—and expensive—item in local markets around the world.
What's it taste like? It has a fatty flavor described as "bacon soup." In fact, each grub's brittle shell turns it into a sort of mini soup can that you can pop into your mouth and swallow, casing and all.

SIDE DISH: GRASSHOPPER

Where it's eaten: Everywhere
How it's prepared: The most commonly eaten insect, grasshoppers are usually fried or roasted and seasoned to taste.
What's it taste like? Spicy popcorn, although—like tofu and rice—grasshoppers tend to take on the flavors of whatever they're cooked with. Their diets affect their taste, too. When katydids (a grasshopper cousin) eat alfalfa, for instance, they taste sweet; katydids that munch on sagebrush taste woody and bland.

MAIN DISH: SCORPIONS

Where it's eaten: Thailand, China, and some neighboring countries
How it's prepared: Sautéed, baked, roasted, and occasionally fried.
What's it taste like? Funky and bitter like spoiled crab meat that has gone bad. Perhaps this side dish is best kept well to the side.

DESSERT: GIANT WATERBUG

Where it's eaten: Southeast Asia
How it's prepared: Fried, roasted, chopped into pieces, or even filleted.
What's it taste like? Although cooked waterbug flesh looks like crab meat, it has a sweet fragrance and an even sweeter flavor, sort of like a Jolly Rancher.

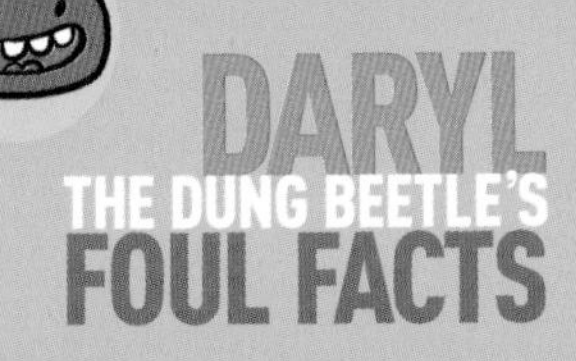

BEFORE YOU LOSE YOUR LUNCH at the thought of a bug banquet, consider this: You already eat about **TWO POUNDS** (.9 kg) of insect bits every year. They're ground into everything you eat during the food-production and packaging processes.

Imagine shoving through some forgotten door in your basement—only to end up in a tunnel lined with ancient bones and grinning skulls! Would you scream? Bolt for the exit? Call the police?

If you lived in Paris, you'd probably go for a stroll. The City of Light sits above a realm of darkness, a never-ending labyrinth of sewers, vaults, wine cellars, canals, and quarries. Explorers risk running into pockets of explosive gas and, rumor has it, monster rats! They're sure to come across Paris' famous crypts. The dead down here outnumber the living in the city above by three to one. Centuries ago, their bones were stacked neatly along the walls in every direction. In the grand scheme of the city's long history, however, these "catacombs" are a new addition.

Plagues, starvation, and wars had filled Paris' cemeteries to the bursting point by the end of the 1700s. Church graveyards were leaking putrid bodies and bits of bone into the basements of nearby restaurants and homes. Think you'd enjoy your dinner in a city that reeked of its rotting dead? In 1785, workers began digging up corpses from the overflowing cemeteries and dumping them into the city's limestone quarries. Thirty years later, six million skeletons had been relocated into these new catacombs. Bones were stacked willy-nilly. Skulls from Parisians who had died more than 1,200 years ago sat atop femurs from casualties of the French Revolution in 1789. With their grave markers long lost, all the bodies were nobodies.

Today, the Catacombs of Paris are a top tourist attraction, but exploring deeper into this underground realm is against the law. That doesn't stop adventurous "cataphiles" from creeping into the darkness through secret doorways and unmarked manholes. They venture down here to party, paint, or just get away from the land of the living.

ombs OF PARIS

ICKY UNDERGROUND

THE FIVE FOULEST THINGS FOUND IN SEWERS

Razor blades, antifreeze, toilet paper, laundry detergent—if it washes down a drain, flows into a gutter, or flushes down the toilet, it ends up in the sewer. Let's pry open a manhole for a peek at the five nastiest things that end up in those pipes and tunnels beneath the street.

5) CRITTERS: The warm and wet environment is a tropical paradise for roaches and rats.

4) COOKING GREASE: Oil dumped from restaurant kitchens coalesces into a clogging fatty goop.

3) CHEMICALS: Storms fill the sewers with a toxic soup washed from the roads.

2) BACTERIA: All the worst germs live down here. Sewer workers who suffer a cut seek immediate treatment.

1) POOP: It's no surprise that number two is number one here. The average adult squeezes out more than 350 pounds (158 kilograms) of poop a year. Add up the annual output of every city dweller and you have a feces tsunami.

Mexican Truffle

SOUNDS LIKE A TREAT!

Truffles are usually one of two things: a flavorful underground mushroom or a kind of chocolate candy. What could be so bad about this Mexican variety?

MORE LIKE A TRICK!

Mexican truffle is just an appetite-friendly name for a kind of fungus that infects corn kernels. This protein-rich delicacy adds an earthy flavor to soups and tortilla dishes, although we doubt many diners would try Mexican truffle if it appeared on the menu under its original Aztec name: "raven excrement."

Treat or Trick?

Scrapple

SOUNDS LIKE A TREAT!

A favorite breakfast treat among the Pennsylvania Dutch—a community that embraces 19th-century living for religious reasons—scrapple sounds like some sort of scrumptious, old-fashioned apple-flavored pastry.

MORE LIKE A TRICK!

The "scrap" in scrapple refers to whatever's left of a butchered hog once all the best parts have been hauled away to the barbecue. Cornmeal mush is added to pork skin, pork heart, pork tongue, pork liver, pork brains, and pork *whatever else is left!* The whole piggy pile is shaped into a loaf and fried. Somehow, we doubt that a dish of scrapple a day keeps the doctor away.

Chocolate Meat

SOUNDS LIKE A TREAT!

Photos of this Filipino stewlike dish—called *dinuguan* in the local language—look downright savory, although "chocolate soup" would make for a tastier-sounding name.

MORE LIKE A TRICK!

Bad news: Dinuguan's chocolate color actually comes from pork blood rather than rich cocoa. The blood serves as a gravy for all manner of pig organs, including lungs, intestines, the heart, and even the snout.

Sweetbread

SOUNDS LIKE A TREAT!

What's to fear from a delicacy called "sweetbread"? A sugar rush, maybe? A raisin stuck in your teeth?

MORE LIKE A TRICK!

Neither sweet nor bread, sweetbreads are actually fried glands (typically, the immunity-boosting thymus gland) or internal organs (such as the pancreas) of cows, pigs, or lambs. Sweetbread lovers claim the dish has a mild flavor similar to brains. Um, yum?

Larvets

SOUNDS LIKE A TREAT!

These extra-crunchy alternatives to chips come festively packaged in three tasty-sounding varieties: BBQ, cheddar cheese, and Mexican spice.

MORE LIKE A TRICK!

Larvets are actually farm-raised insect larvae from Hotlix, makers of "the original candy that bugs." Other crunchy Hotlix treats include Scorpion Suckers and Cricket Lick-Its.

CRUNCH TIME

EIGHTY PERCENT of the world's population includes **INSECTS** as a regular part of their **DIET.**

DOG POUND

Americans eat **7 BILLION HOT DOGS** every summer. That's a lot of mechanically separated poultry and sodium erythorbate!

WASTING AWAY

The average American tosses out more than **4 POUNDS** (2 kg) of **GARBAGE** each day.

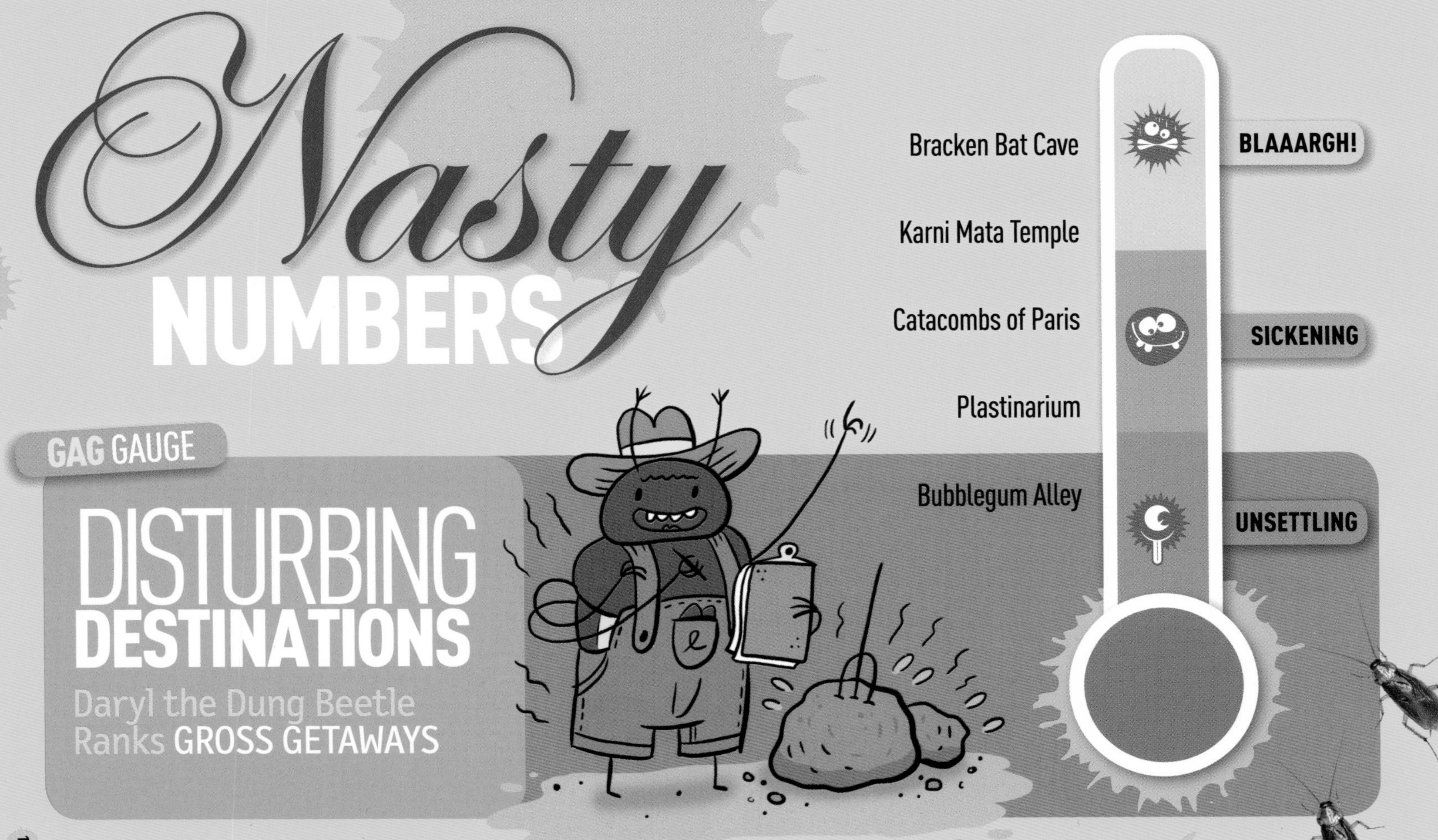
Nasty NUMBERS
GAG GAUGE
DISTURBING DESTINATIONS
Daryl the Dung Beetle Ranks GROSS GETAWAYS
Bracken Bat Cave
Karni Mata Temple
Catacombs of Paris
Plastinarium
Bubblegum Alley
BLAAARGH!
SICKENING
UNSETTLING

CHAPTER 6

Shocking Pop Culture

GROSS SELLS. NEED PROOF? Just look at the top-ten blockbuster movies of all time! *Star Wars* (fourth on the list) shows us an entire cantina of creepy aliens. *Shrek 2* (in fifth place) stars a grotesque green monster who passes gas. And *Titanic* (number two) is nothing but yucky smooching scenes on a sinking ship. Ick, ick, ick! For every pop star who makes us go gaga, there's a movie monster that grosses us out. This chapter is dedicated to all the freaky shows, the awful arts, and the sickening pastimes that make us scream!

THE ACK!-ADEMY AWARDS!

We Honor Hollywood's Most Disgusting Stars and Scenes

CREEPIEST CLAYMATION

OOGIE BOOGIE

AS SEEN IN: *THE NIGHTMARE BEFORE CHRISTMAS*
A Santa-swiping body bag with a bad attitude, Oogie Boogie is easily the most horrid inhabitant of Halloween Town.

NASTIEST SCENE: Lanky hero Jack Skellington yanks a loose string to unravel Oogie Boogie's body—revealing a writhing mass of worms and insects!

SLIMIEST SPACE ALIEN

JABBA THE HUTT

AS SEEN IN: *STAR WARS: RETURN OF THE JEDI*
A ruthless galactic gangster with the body of a slug and the face of a frog, Jabba captures poor Princess Leia and encases roguish Han Solo in a prison of carbonite.

NASTIEST SCENE: When Jabba slurps down a live toad, then licks the spittle from his slimy lips.

MOST HORRIBLE HERO

AS SEEN IN: *SHREK*
This crude ogre uses his repulsive powers—including flammable burps and intense body odor—to rescue a princess.

NASTIEST SCENE: Shrek fashions candles out of his own earwax.

VILEST VILLAIN

AS SEEN IN: THE *HARRY POTTER* MOVIES

This power-hungry wizard embodies ultimate evil in the magical world of Harry Potter, and he has a face to match. With his flattened nose and snakelike slits for nostrils, "He-Who-Must-Not-Be-Named" oozes ill intent.

NASTIEST SCENE: Professor Quirinus Quirrell unwraps his turban at the end of *Harry Potter and the Sorcerer's Stone* to reveal a reborn Voldemort hatching from the back of his head!

LORD VOLDEMORT

THE CHEESE TOUCH

NASTIEST SNACK

AS SEEN IN: *DIARY OF A WIMPY KID*

Left to rot on a middle school basketball court for years, a moldy slice of Swiss cheese has become a legend among the students. It curses anyone who touches it!

NASTIEST SCENE: One unlucky kid has to peel the sickening slice off the ground and eat it.

AUGUSTUS GLOOP

MESSIEST EATER

AS SEEN IN: *CHARLIE AND THE CHOCOLATE FACTORY*

A big boy with a superhuman sweet tooth, Augustus wins a tour of Willy Wonka's Chocolate Factory. It doesn't take long for his bottomless appetite to land him in deep trouble!

NASTIEST SCENE: While being interviewed by TV reporters, Augustus crams a candy bar into his mouth—smearing half his face with chocolate in the processs!

Eww 'TOONS!

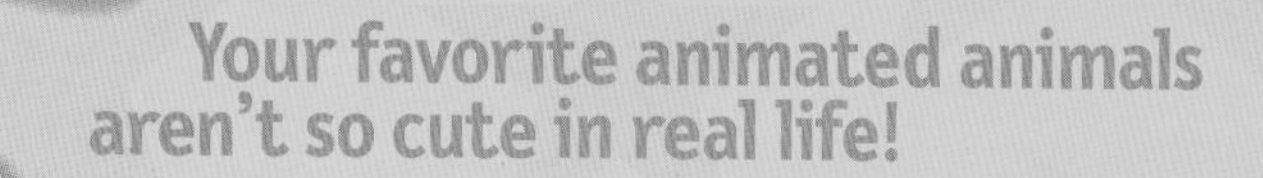

Your favorite animated animals aren't so cute in real life!

AMOEBA BOYS
(THE POWERPUFF GIRLS)

IN THE CARTOON: These microscopic mobsters plot big-time crimes, but their itty-bitty brains are too primitive to pull off any caper more complicated than grand theft orange.
IN REAL LIFE: Amoebas are single-celled blobs of protoplasm that swim or crawl using gooey arms. Most are microscopic, but some deep-sea amoebas grow larger than your finger!
THE UGLY TRUTH: Some amoebas live in bodies of water; others live inside human bodies. The fearsome parasitic *Naegleria fowleri*—better known as the "brain-eating amoeba"—lurks in lakes, rivers, and even swimming pools. It has killed several people after swimming up their noses and gorging on their gray matter.

PATRICK STAR
(SPONGEBOB SQUAREPANTS)

IN THE CARTOON: This brainless pink seastar mopes around the town of Bikini Bottom, latching on to his buddy SpongeBob for stuff to do.
IN REAL LIFE: Literally brainless (and even headless!), starfish mope around the ocean bottom, latching on to prey with more than a thousand tiny sucker feet.
THE UGLY TRUTH: Some starfish barf their stomachs from their mouths to digest food outside their bodies before sucking the whole mess back in. That's what I call going out for dinner!

IN THE CARTOON: Fed up with eating garbage from the sewers of Paris, this sophisticated rodent sneaks into a French restaurant and learns the art of gourmet cooking.
IN REAL LIFE: Known as "domestic rodents" for their long history of pestering people, rats will gladly devour five-star French food—along with any other edible garbage they find in the alley Dumpster. Rats have even been known to bite babies in their cribs!
THE UGLY TRUTH: Through their bite, fleas, and feces dropped in human food, rats have spread some of history's most diabolical diseases!

REMY
(RATATOUILLE)

MUMBLE
(HAPPY FEET)

IN THE CARTOON: This young, tap-dancing emperor penguin embarks on a toe-tapping quest to learn why all the fish are disappearing from Antarctica. It turns out overfishing by humans is to blame.
IN REAL LIFE: Real emperor penguins may not cut a rug, but they face the same dilemmas as Mumble and his buddies. Commercial fishing takes a huge toll on the penguins' food supply, while climate change is melting their icy habitat.
THE UGLY TRUTH: Like little poop-squirting Super Soakers, Adélie penguins can shoot their droppings more than a foot (30.5 cm) from their rocky nests. Hey, you'd projectile poop, too, if you didn't want to leave your warm nest to go potty in subzero temperatures!

DARYL THE DUNG BEETLE'S FOUL FACTS

NOT ALL RODENTS ARE ROTTEN!
The rough-and-tumble grasshopper mouse takes on scorpions, centipedes, and tarantulas, dodging their stingers and fangs like a kung fu rodent. It even unleashes a **BATTLE SHRIEK** before it attacks. My hero!

PLOP CULTURE

ART IMITATES LIFE WITH CLOACA: THE **ICKY** EATING MACHINE!

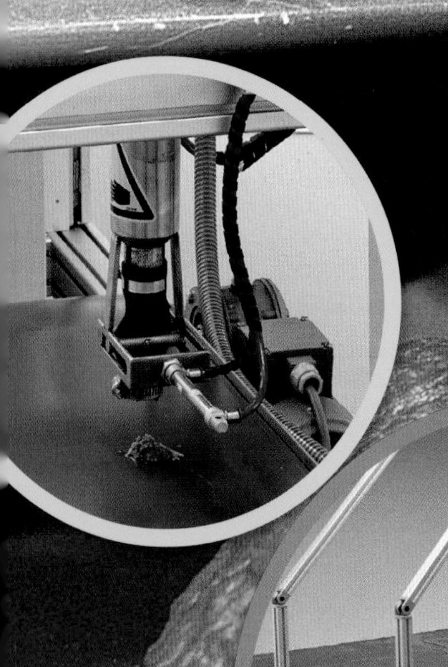

FEEDING TIME IS SOMETHING YOU'D EXPECT TO SEE AT A ZOO, NOT AN ART MUSEUM. Nevertheless, twice a day, attendants at Tasmania's Museum of Old and New Art dump gourmet dishes into Cloaca, a room-size contraption of interconnected tubes, bile-filled bags, and chemical vats all kept at the temperature of a human body. Twenty-seven hours later, a pungent brown paste squirts from Cloaca's opposite end in revolting swirls upon a revolving table.

This process sound familiar? Yes, Cloaca is a machine that turns food into poop. It's actually the latest in a series of digestion engines created by Belgian artist Wim Delvoye, whose invention gets loads of attention at every museum that hosts it. Visitors line up to snap photos, stick their fingers into Cloaca's poo, and even buy some artificial feces—which certainly smells like the real deal!

Delvoye spent years collaborating with scientists to make certain his poop factory mimicked every stage of human food processing. Blenders in Cloaca's food basin chew each meal. Acid in its stomach container breaks down the food so that bacteria in the phony colon can finish the job. The bacteria even produce gas just like the microbes in your digestive tract. That's right—Cloaca is art that toots!

DARYL THE DUNG BEETLE'S FOUL FACTS

MUSEUM VISITORS can buy authentic Cloaca poops for **$1,000** a piece. Say, did you know my birthday's next week? Hint, hint!

BOG SNORKELING 1

THE GIST: Chilly, remote, and with the soupy consistency of diarrhea, the Waen Rhydd peat bog in Wales is about as enticing a swimming hole as your local sewage-treatment plant. Oh, and if you recall from chapter 1, these murky swamps are notorious hidey holes for long-forgotten corpses. None of these disgusting details deter silly snorkelers from gearing up every August for the World Bog Snorkeling Championships.

THE GEAR: Swimming fins, mask and snorkel, and a wetsuit. Wacky superhero costume optional.

THE GUIDELINES: Snorkelers take turns making a round-trip swim along a 60-yard (54.9 m) trench of bog water. As if racing through zero-visibility muck wasn't tough enough, the contestants aren't allowed to use their arms!

SiCKENING SPORTS

FiVE PASTiMES THAT MIGHT MAKE YOU PUKE

WORM CHARMING 2

THE GIST: Perhaps the only activity in which the words "worms" and "charming" make sense together, worm charming is the art of coaxing squiggling armies of slimy earthworms from the muddy ground using nothing but sound. Charmers compete every summer at the World Worm-Charming Championships, held in the soggy English countryside. (A similar "Worm Gruntin' Festival" takes place each April in Sopchoppy, Florida.) By the end of a typical competition, the ground is absolutely oozing with slippery dirt-covered nightcrawlers!

THE GEAR: Pitchforks, knitting needles, subwoofers, musical instruments, homemade vibration-generating contraptions—any tool that woos worms from the earth using vibration alone.

THE GUIDELINES: Working in two-person teams, competitors have 30 minutes to charm as many worms as they can from a roughly nine-square-foot (one-square-meter) plot of earth. Worm catchers must pluck with care; crawlers broken into icky bits don't count toward the total!

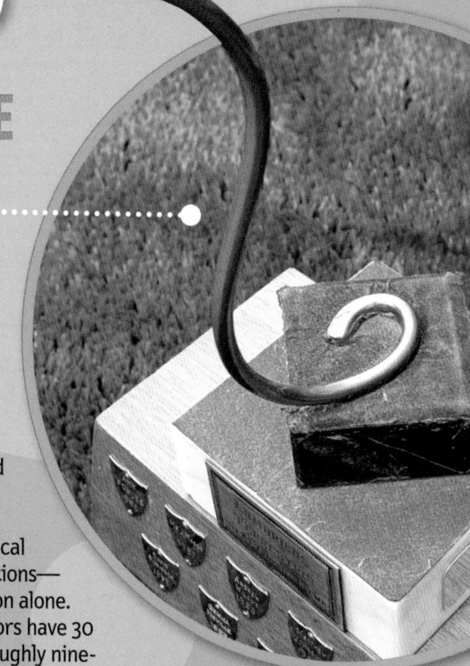

3 COCKROACH RACING

THE GIST: Buckets of squirming roaches—each individually numbered and given names like "Lord of the Drains" and "Ita Buttroach"—are sent scurrying as a spectator sport at Brisbane's Story Bridge Hotel. Roaches compete in various themed races, including hurdling events in which the bugs have to clamber over garden hoses.

THE GEAR: Roach racers can bring their own bugs or buy them for $5 each.

THE GUIDELINES: Each race begins when a referee empties a bucket of roaches in the center of a boxing ring. Roach wranglers scoop up the first bug to leave the ring and declare it the winner. Performance-enhancing substances such as sugar and coffee are strictly forbidden.

4 COW-CHIP TOSSING

THE GIST: In case you hadn't guessed, "cow chip" is just a tasteful term for "cow plops." And for whatever reason, people like tossing these disgusting discs up and away with their bare hands. The globe's best chip chuckers gather every April in Beaver, Oklahoma, for the World Championship Cow-Chip Throw. You'll know you're in the right place when you spot the giant fiberglass beaver clutching a cow patty at the tourney grounds.

THE GEAR: Projectiles of sun-dried cow poop at least 6 inches (15 cm) in diameter, selected from an official chip wagon that's guarded around the clock to prevent poop tampering.

THE GUIDELINES: Competitors get two chips to toss however they like as long as they don't cross the foul line.

5 COMPETITIVE EATING

THE GIST: Under a time limit, "gastro-athletes" cram their bottomless bellies with whatever's on the contest menu: chicken wings, hard-boiled eggs, jalapeños, even mayonnaise! Despite training their stomachs to stretch beyond doctor-approved limits, many pro eaters still experience disqualifying "reversals" in the heat of competition. Which means, they don't just lose—they lose their lunch!

THE GEAR: A hearty appetite and a bowl of liquid, in which competitors dip doughy foods so they slide down easier.

THE GUIDELINES: At the annual Nathan's Famous hot-dog-eating championship, the Super Bowl of competitive eating, gastro-athletes have ten minutes to devour as many hot dogs as possible. They're allowed to snap the dogs in half and soak the buns in water—which makes for sloppy eating despite penalties for messiness. The world record is 68 hot dogs. Do *not* try that at home!

HUNGRY FOR MORE patty-related pastimes? Try "cowpat bingo." This popular fundraising activity has **COWS POOPING** onto a grassy grid that matches players' bingo cards. Sounds delicious!

DARYL THE DUNG BEETLE'S FOUL FACTS

Zombies!

Vampires are too busy pouting and looking pretty. Werewolves have lost their old-world creepiness. Witches and warlocks are more heroic than hideous. Let's face it: Movie monsters aren't what they used to be. But at least we can count on one crowd of creatures to maintain their repulsive image: zombies! They shamble! They stink! They want to eat our brains!

With the release of the 1968 horror movie *Night of the Living Dead*, zombies—the most disgusting monsters to crawl from Hollywood—became pop culture icons. They're walking corpses, after all, half rotten and literally smelling like death warmed over. Now imagine one of these bloated, maggot-eaten monsters stumbling after you, its dirty fingers clawing for your flesh. Slow but never tiring, a zombie will catch you sooner or later. And once it sinks its

teeth into your tender skin, you'll become a zombie, too. More than just foul, zombies are infectious!

African and Haitian history is filled with folklore of voodoo priests using sorcery and supernatural substances to resurrect the recently deceased and turn them into zonked-out slaves. The most famous zombie of all was Clairvius Narcisse, a Haitian man declared dead (and even buried!) in 1962. It turns out he had been poisoned by his brother to appear deceased, then dug up and forced to work on a plantation under the effects of mind-controlling chemicals. Eventually, the drugs wore off and Narcisse escaped. He wasn't rotten or reaching for brains when he returned to his home village in 1980, but his sister still screamed at the sight of him. For all she knew, he had been dead for nearly 20 years!

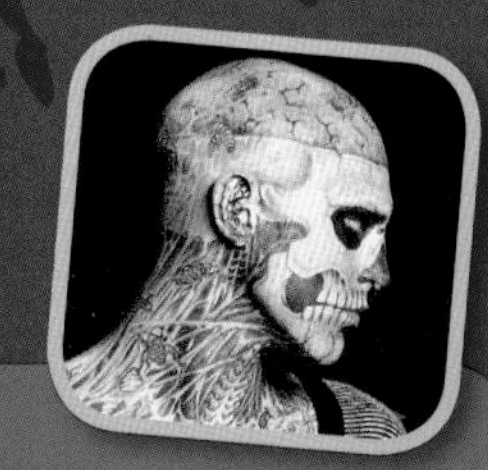

Inspired by his favorite horror flicks, Canadian model **RICK GENEST** spent six years covering his body with intricate tattoos that depict his own decomposition. In a way, he's become a living zombie!

MIKE THE ZOMBIE CHICKEN

Originally bound for the dinner table, Mike the chicken lost his head to a farmer's axe in 1945—but he didn't lose his life! Unfazed by his beheading, the chicken hopped right off the chopping block and resumed pecking for corn with his bloody stump of a neck. The farmer's axe had hacked off Mike's head but left behind just enough brain stem for Mike to resume his daily routine of preening and eating.

Once the farmer realized he could keep Mike alive by squirting food down his throat with an eyedropper, the headless chicken became a celebrity. He toured in sideshows and posed for magazines until he finally passed away 18 months later. Today, the beheaded bird's legacy lives on with an annual Mike the Headless Chicken Day in his hometown of Fruita, Colorado.

DARYL THE DUNG BEETLE'S FOUL FACTS

BEFORE THE INVENTION of modern medical sensors, doctors relied on all kinds of **HORRIBLE METHODS** to make sure people were actually dead before they could be buried, including prodding them with hot pokers and pouring pee into their mouths!

9 FEET, 2 INCHES (2.8 M)

THE DISTANCE RECORD FOR **SQUIRTING MILK** FROM THE HUMAN EYE

REPULSIVE RECORDS

IMAGINE TRYING TO BEAT THESE FOUL FEATS!

THE LONGEST AMOUNT OF TIME SPENT LIVING IN A **ROOM FILLED WITH SCORPIONS** —MORE THAN 5,000 OF THEM!

33 DAYS

16

THE MOST HISSING **COCKROACHES** EVER CRAMMED INTO SOMEONE'S MOUTH

28 FEET, 4 INCHES
(8.6 M)

THE LENGTH OF THE WORLD'S LONGEST **FINGERNAILS**

17.7 POUNDS
(8 KG)

THE LARGEST AMOUNT OF **COW BRAINS** DEVOURED IN AN EATING COMPETITION IN 15 MINUTES

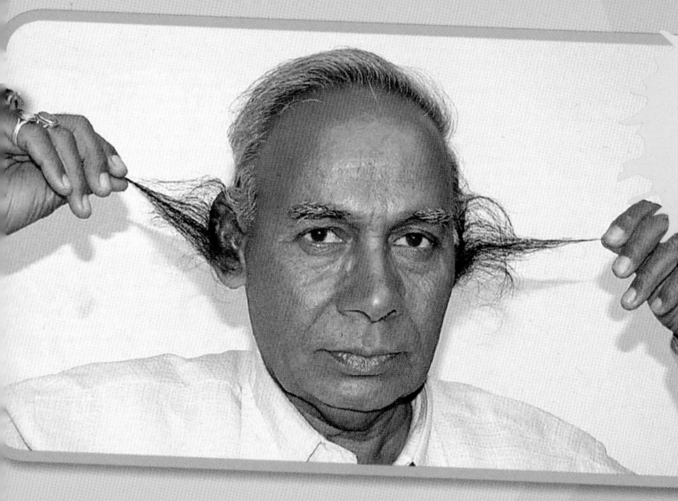

7.12 INCHES
(18.2 CM)

THE LENGTH OF THE LONGEST **EAR HAIR**

PIMPLE POPPER

Depicting a volcanic zit at the moment of eruption, the Pimple Popper ring just begs for a good squeezing. This repulsively realistic piece of jewelry is wrought of silver and copper coated in glassy enamel. A freshwater pearl—one of nature's most beautiful gemstones—serves as the pus-packed whitehead. The one-of-a-kind ring sold for $163, but don't fret if you still want to decorate your finger with a facial blemish. Artist Winona Johnson hopes her Pimple Popper will be just the first in a series of skin-related jewelry.

OFF-THE-WALL ART

Exhibits That Make You Go "Eww"!

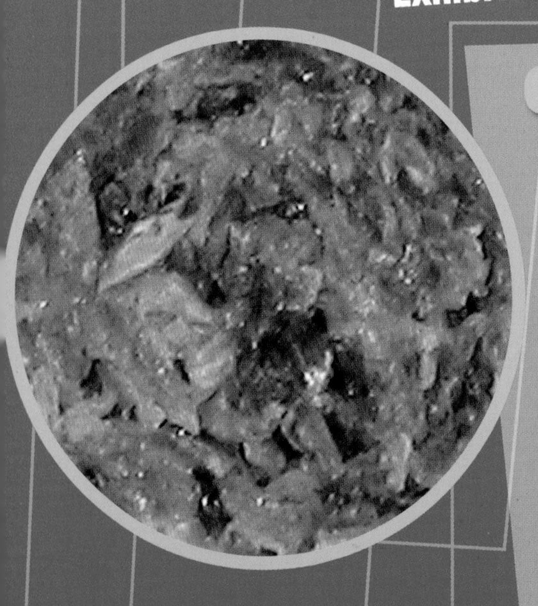

SNOT BALL

When his college buddy argued that even a ball of boogers could pass for modern art, English artist James Ford set about picking a winner. He dug deep for two years and molded his dried-up snot into the "Bogey Ball," a round mound of mucus about the size of a Brussels sprout. This orb of green goo gained fame in several gallery displays, and Ford eventually offered to sell it for about $20,000. He got no takers, but don't let that stop you from molding mucus for fun rather than profit. Ford's advice for aspiring snot artists: Pick a mix of dry and wet boogers for the sturdiest ball. "Think of dry mucus as the bricks," he says, "and the sticky snot as the mortar."

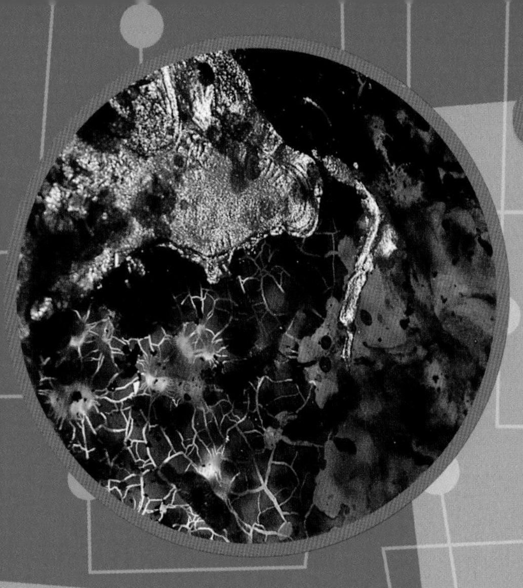

SEEING RED

The paintings of New York artist Jordan Eagles bring to mind Martian landscapes, tongues of flame, and microscopic organisms. They take on new meaning when you learn of his secret ingredient: cow blood recycled from slaughterhouses. Working in a steamy studio so that his "paint" doesn't scab up, Eagles sandwiches the blood between transparent sheets of plasticlike material. He adds copper for extra vibrancy and then tries other tricks gleaned from more than a decade spent working with the red stuff. The end result is haunting proof that even blood can be beautiful.

BODY ART

Yanked teeth, clipped nails, and locks of lost hair go from being repulsive to posh in the hands of Australian artist Polly van der Glas, who cleans up these cast-off body bits before setting them in precious metal. She molds molars into earrings, fashions necklace charms out of nail clippings, and weaves hair into knuckle guards. Word has it the Tooth Fairy is her biggest fan!

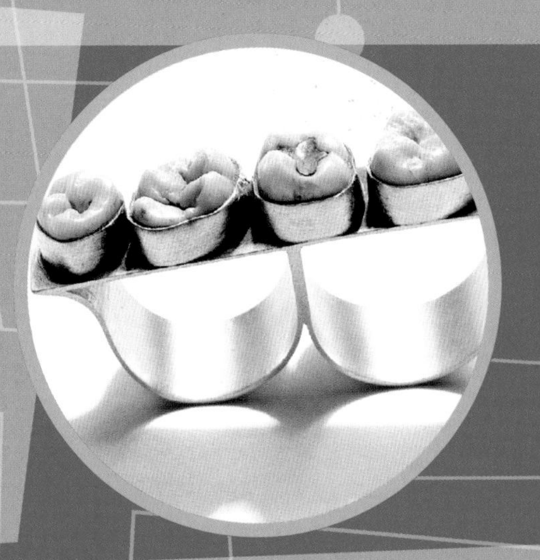

HAIRY LEGS

Insects are already creepy enough. Now imagine an entire swarm fashioned from human hair! Seattle artist Adrienne Antonson specializes in sculpting bugs from her own silky strands, along with follicles from friends and family. Mixing the hair with glue, she's managed to mold more than 40 insects—everything from bees to beetles to caterpillar cocoons. They might sound scary, but these hairy creations are surprisingly pretty and colorful. Antonson plans to create even more insects, and why not? Unlike sculptors who work with wood or marble, she can grow her own moldable material for free!

SKUNK**APE**

This Florida version of **BIGFOOT** supposedly smells like a mixture of rotten eggs, cow poop, and a wet dog that's never gotten a bath.

CHUPACABRA

Spanish for **"GOAT SUCKER,"** this mythical monster allegedly creeps into barnyards to suck the blood of livestock. Scientists who studied supposed chupacabra corpses determined they were actually mangy coyotes.

KAPPA

Next time you accidentally make some bubbles at the local swimming hole, blame it on the kappa. According to legend, this Japanese **WATER MONSTER** loves passing gas!

Loathsome LEGENDS

GAG GAUGE

MONSTERS!

Daryl the Dung Beetle Ranks Our Featured **CREATURES**

CHAPTER 7

Everyday Grossness

DON'T BOTHER LOCKING YOUR DOORS.

Closing your windows won't do any good. Your home sweet home is already a haven for the forces of foulness. You think your toilet seat is grody? Or your laundry hamper? Then do yourself a favor: Never look at your toothbrush under a microscope! In fact, you might just want to skip this chapter altogether. Turns out you never have to wander far to find grossness. It's all around you!

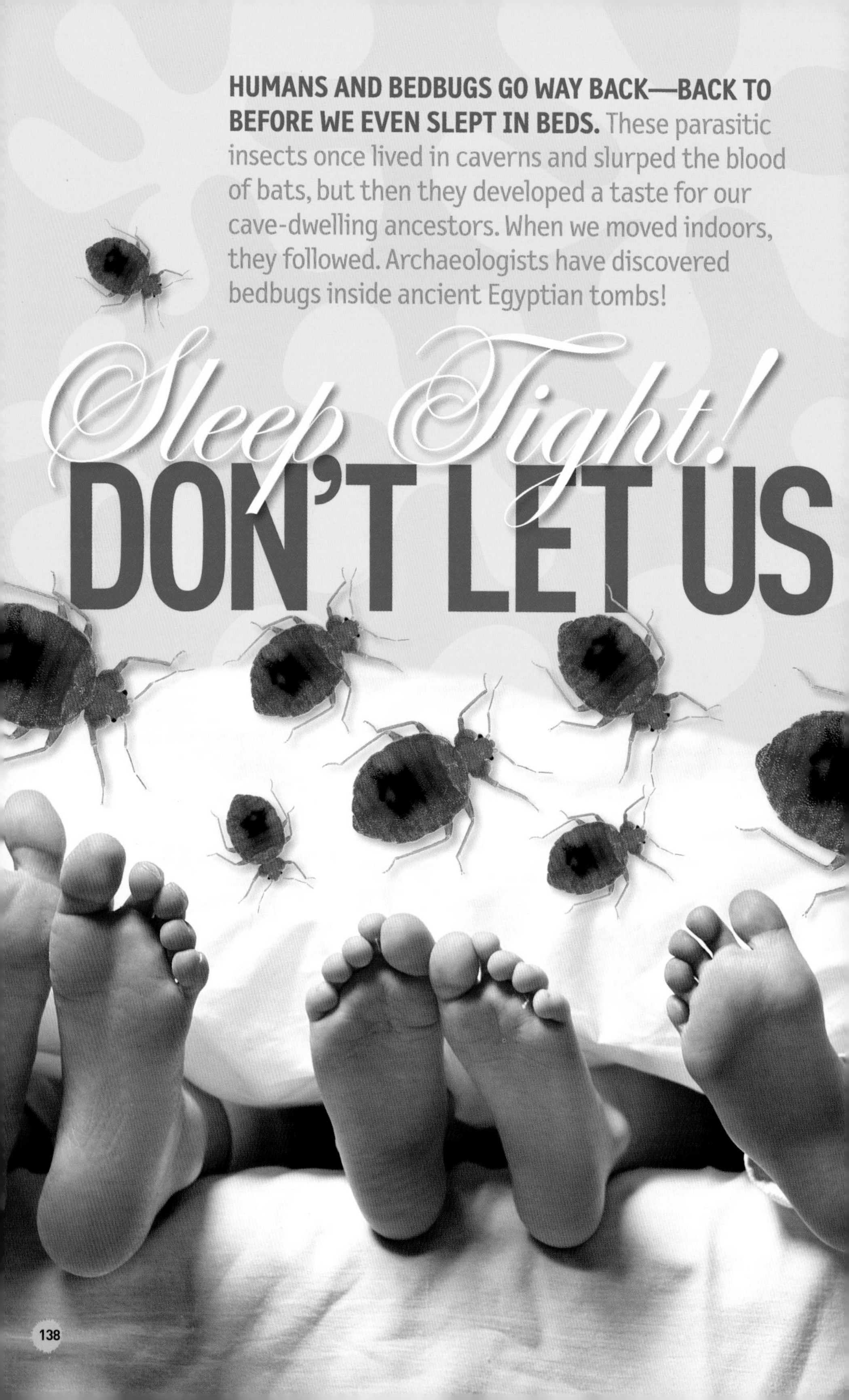

HUMANS AND BEDBUGS GO WAY BACK—BACK TO BEFORE WE EVEN SLEPT IN BEDS. These parasitic insects once lived in caverns and slurped the blood of bats, but then they developed a taste for our cave-dwelling ancestors. When we moved indoors, they followed. Archaeologists have discovered bedbugs inside ancient Egyptian tombs!

Sleep Tight! DON'T LET US

With flat bodies made for squeezing through the teensiest cracks, bedbugs are nearly unstoppable in their quest for blood. It's all they eat! They can track down your bedroom by sensing the carbon dioxide in your breath. By day, the tiny bugs hunker down in the box spring below your mattress, just waiting for your warm-blooded body to hit the sack. Then, it's time for a midnight snack! They belly up to your skin and start drilling for blood, releasing an anesthetic so you don't notice the bite. Once they've drunk their fill, bedbugs scurry back to the box spring before sunrise. Their bites don't spread disease, but the itchy welts they leave behind reveal a scary message: You're not sleeping alone!

BiTE!

SO LONG, SUCKERS!

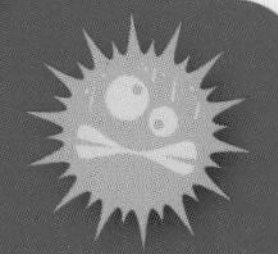

Nearly exterminated half a century ago, bedbugs are making a comeback—especially in hotels and apartment buildings. Keeping these bloodsuckers out of your bed isn't too tricky if you follow this advice:

- Set your luggage on a table or suitcase rack when you travel. Don't leave it on the floor.
- Inspect hotel beds for signs of infestation, such as red or brown spots on the linens. Check the corners of your mattress for the tiny bugs.
- Leave your luggage outside for a day when you get home from your travels.
- Wash all your clothes as soon as you return home. Run anything that might be infested through the dryer.

IF LEFT UNCHECKED, thousands of bedbugs can infest a single bedroom, biting on their sleeping victims more than **500 times** each *night*!

DARYL THE DUNG BEETLE'S FOUL FACTS

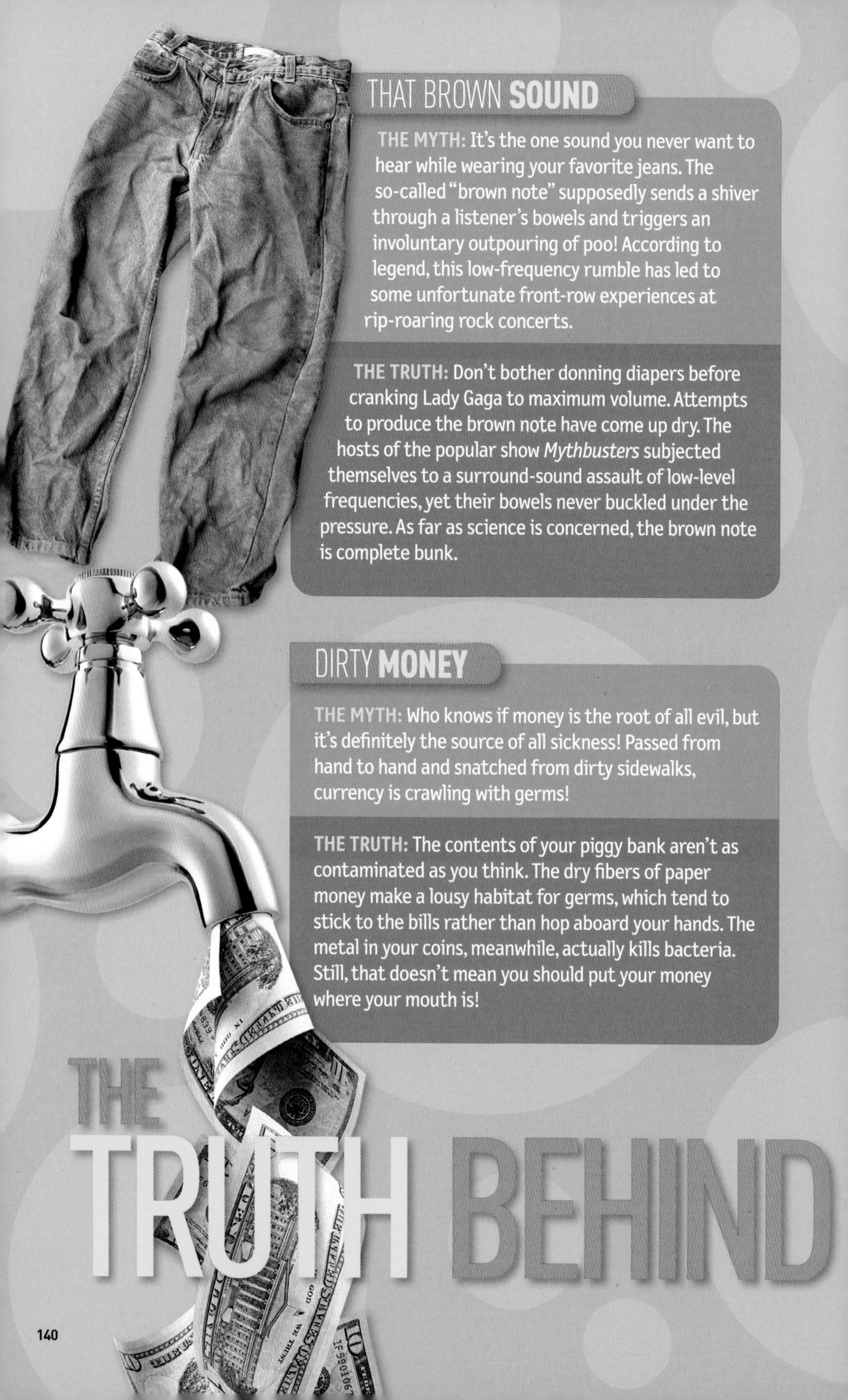

THAT BROWN **SOUND**

THE MYTH: It's the one sound you never want to hear while wearing your favorite jeans. The so-called "brown note" supposedly sends a shiver through a listener's bowels and triggers an involuntary outpouring of poo! According to legend, this low-frequency rumble has led to some unfortunate front-row experiences at rip-roaring rock concerts.

THE TRUTH: Don't bother donning diapers before cranking Lady Gaga to maximum volume. Attempts to produce the brown note have come up dry. The hosts of the popular show *Mythbusters* subjected themselves to a surround-sound assault of low-level frequencies, yet their bowels never buckled under the pressure. As far as science is concerned, the brown note is complete bunk.

DIRTY **MONEY**

THE MYTH: Who knows if money is the root of all evil, but it's definitely the source of all sickness! Passed from hand to hand and snatched from dirty sidewalks, currency is crawling with germs!

THE TRUTH: The contents of your piggy bank aren't as contaminated as you think. The dry fibers of paper money make a lousy habitat for germs, which tend to stick to the bills rather than hop aboard your hands. The metal in your coins, meanwhile, actually kills bacteria. Still, that doesn't mean you should put your money where your mouth is!

THE TRUTH BEHIND

GUMMED-UP **GUTS**

THE MYTH: Don't swallow your gum unless you want it sticking with you—for seven years! That's a lesson straight from Mom, who warned that gum doesn't digest; it just sits in your stomach soaking in a stew of digestive juices and taking up space.

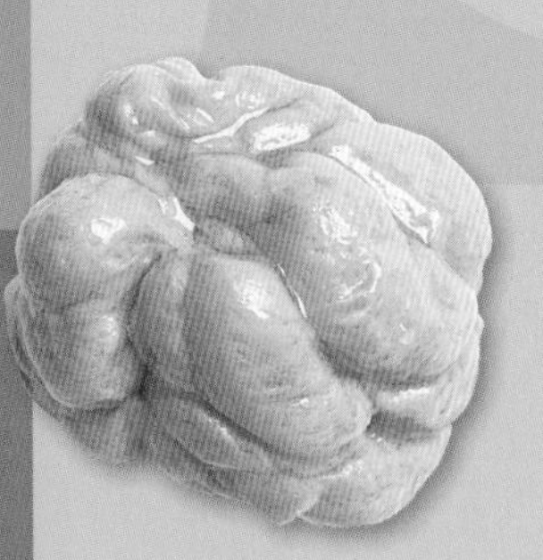

THE TRUTH: Acids and enzymes in your belly make short work of gum's sugars and flavor additives, but its synthetic-rubber base is one tough glob to digest. That doesn't mean gum just swirls around and around in your inner works like a penny in a washing machine. Your stomach regularly empties its contents into the intestine for further digestion. Any gum gobs, corn kernels, or other tough-to-digest treats go along for the ride. It all gets pushed to the colon and passed in your poop, looking much as it did when you ate it. Not that we suggest you go looking...

THE FIVE-SECOND **RULE**

THE MYTH: No one sets out to eat off the floor, but what choice do you have when you get a case of the butterfingers while munching on a Butterfinger? No worries! Just scoop it up before the germs have a chance to hop aboard. After all, desperate times call for desperate measures, and you have five seconds to react, right? *Right?*

THE TRUTH: Scientists who study germs think the five-second rule should be renamed the *no-second* rule. Bacteria on the floor cling to fallen food immediately, and your gut reaction to rescue toppled treats might lead to some unfortunate reactions in your guts. "If your food lands in a place where the dog poops, it doesn't make a difference how quickly you pick it up," says germ expert Dr. Charles Gerba. "It is still going to have fecal bacteria on it."

MESSY MYTHS

YOUR POOPY TOOTHBRUSH

Sickening germs, viruses, and even fungi can thrive on your toothbrush's damp bristles. You're best off letting it dry completely between uses—and never, ever sharing it!

WHOOSH! Few sounds are more reassuring than a toilet's flush. After all, you're sending the stinky stuff in the bowl to the icky depths of the sewer where it belongs. But pushing that shiny handle comes with nasty consequences for everything in the bathroom—particularly your toothbrush!

The swirling action of a toilet's flush turns some of the bowl's sewage into airborne poo. In other words, what goes down also comes up in the form of tiny droplets. This flush-propelled fog is packed with poop particles, urine, viruses, and bacteria. It can travel several feet and linger in the air for more than two hours after each flush!

If your toothbrush sits in the splash zone—and chances are it does—then you've been brushing your teeth with more than just toothpaste! The good news is bacteria and viruses can't survive on your brush once the bristles dry, and micro-bits of fecal matter won't hurt anyone with a healthy immune system. Still, unless you're okay with sticking a poopy toothbrush into your mouth, you should close the toilet's lid before each flush.

YOUR DiRTY LAUNDRY

YOUR COMMODE isn't the only contraption that spreads feces far and wide. Surprisingly enough, the family washing machine is another culprit. The instant you toss dirty undies into the washer's soapy broth, the machine becomes a cauldron of fecal contamination. "If you do undergarments in one load and handkerchiefs in the next," says microbiologist Dr. Charles Gerba, "you're blowing your nose in what was in your underwear." To keep the skid marks on your shorts from fouling your shirts and sheets, save the underwear load for last.

YOUR KiTCHEN

Fido might be on to something when he drinks from the toilet. Studies show that your kitchen is crawling with more bacteria than your commode. The toilet seat is actually a cleaner surface for sandwich making than the kitchen counter! Hold on to your lunch as we reveal the dirty truth behind the most wretched room in your house.

1 COUNTERTOPS

Hey, neat freaks—quit cleaning kitchen counters with the dish sponge! You're only spreading germs across the same surface where you cool cookies and assemble sandwiches. People who wipe their counters less often actually have cleaner kitchens!

2 DiSH SPONGE

Perpetually damp and full of crannies, the dish sponge is like Disneyland for germs. Billions of bacteria—picked up from any raw meat prepared nearby—thrive in the sponge's dark pockets, making it the most awful indoor object. Germs like salmonella and E. coli can trigger vomiting and diarrhea if they get into your stomach, so nuke that sponge in the microwave for 30 seconds to zap all the microbial meanies.

3 KiTCHEN SiNK

"There are usually more fecal bacteria in a kitchen sink than a toilet after you flush it," Dr. Gerba says. Most of those microbes hang out in the icky dampness of the drain, usually out of reach of your food and fingers, but you should still ask a parental unit to sanitize the sink with bleach once in a while.

4 REFRiGERATOR HANDLE

No surprises here. Your hands spread germs to everything they touch, including door handles. The fridge handle is actually germier than the door of a public restroom. How is that possible? People usually wash their hands before leaving the bathroom. The fridge handle gets no such respect.

5 CUTTiNG BOARD

Germs feel right at home in the knife-inflicted nicks of the cutting board, which is actually more contaminated than your kitchen floor! A typical chopping block is home to 200 times more poo-related bacteria than a toilet seat. These germs hitch a ride on veggies and meat, especially chicken! Be sure to run the cutting board through the dishwasher after preparing poultry.

6 COCKROACHES

Uh-oh. If you spot one roach scurrying for cover when you flip on the lights, chances are it has company in the walls. There's a reason these ugly bugs have been around for 350 million years—they're tough and will eat just about anything (including human sweat and eyelashes). Roach poop can trigger asthma and cause other illnesses. Oh, and roaches are frequent gas passers, too. Have you called the exterminator yet?

MONSTER MiTES!

Ever believe that monsters lurk under your bed? Oh, silly you—they lurk *in* your bed. And in your carpet, on your furniture, and even in Spot's sleeping spot. They're called dust mites, and they want to eat your skin!

IT'S A GOOD THING THESE ARACHNIDS ARE TOO TINY TO SEE, BECAUSE DUST MITES ARE *UGLY* LITTLE BUGGERS. They're also just the right size to munch on the millions of dead skin cells you shed every day. A lot of that skin sloughs off in your bedroom, because you spend so much time there. It gets caught in your sheets, blankets, and pillows, creating a dead-skin smorgasbord for dust mites. More than a million live in your bed alone!

Although dust mites don't bite, they can be harmful in other ways. They poop and shed their shells like other arthropods. We stir up dust clouds of their excrement and exoskeletons every time we clean. Inhaling these particles is more than just disgusting—it can trigger allergies and asthma attacks. But dust mites aren't all bad. Without them, our fallen flakes would pile up ankle-deep. And consider this: A study in England showed that leaving your bed unmade might cut down on its colonies of mites. With the blankets cast aside, the sheets underneath lose moisture that the mites need to absorb, so they dry up and die. Wait, did science just give you permission to leave a messy bed? Good luck convincing Mom of that one!

DARYL THE DUNG BEETLE'S FOUL FACTS

DUST MOTES dancing in a sunbeam might look pretty—until you realize that **80 PERCENT** of that debris is actually shed dead skin!

Gross ENCOUNTERS

EVERYDAY OBJECTS THAT ARE SECRETLY DISGUSTING

SOCCER BALLS

"Most soccer balls we tested had fecal bacteria on them," says germ expert Dr. Charles Gerba. Think about that the next time you go in for a header!

TRAIN AND BUS SEATS

Bacteria blossom on public transportation. Take, for instance, the cushy cloth seats of San Francisco's commuter-rail system. Studies revealed a world of fecal bacteria, mold, and hard-to-kill germs living in the food-stained fabric.

AIRPLANE SINKS

Despite rare cases of illness leaping from passenger to passenger, sickness generally doesn't spread in the recycled air of airplanes. It's the bathrooms you have to worry about. Airplane toilets have a jet-powered flush that sprays that funky blue-tinted water—and germs—everywhere. Faucet handles take the brunt of the bacteria, and good luck cleaning your hands in that tiny sink!

BOOKS

Hey, why is the punctuation in your *Harry Potter* novel prancing off the page? That's not a magical comma—it's a book louse! Similar in size and shape to head lice, these bugs snack on the glue binding old books. Book lice don't bite or hop into your hair, but they still make for a nasty surprise in any novel.

SWING SETS

Kids do more than just shout "Whee!" on the swings. Scientists studying playground equipment found traces of wee, poop, snot, and blood.

DARYL THE DUNG BEETLE'S FOUL FACTS

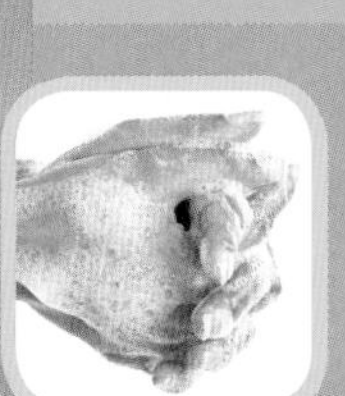

YOUR IMMUNE SYSTEM can contend with most germs, but it's always a good idea to **SCRUB YOUR HANDS** with soap and water before eating or touching your face. Bet you never thought you'd be taking hygiene advice from a dung beetle!

Nice Uses for NASTY THINGS

GRUBBY MEDICINE

Modern doctors have resumed the age-old practice of using maggots for medical procedures—except with some up-to-date twists. Because they only munch on dead tissue, maggots make the perfect cleanup crew for wounds infected with rot. Doctors create a cagelike bandage full of disinfected maggots, which are applied to the injury and allowed to nibble away until only healthy tissue remains. Hey, maybe those ancient healers were on to something!

GROSS FOR THE GREATER GOOD

HORNET JUICE

The Asian giant hornet you saw buzzing around page 84 is more than just a stinging sensation. Able to zoom at 25 mph (40 kph) up to 60 miles (97 km) a day, this big bug is the super-athlete of the insect world. Sports-drink companies have studied the hornet's never-ending endurance and developed a juice from the sticky fluid secreted by the insect's larvae. Olympic athletes chug the bug drink for extra pep, which just goes to show that some people will do anything for a gold medal!

VERSATILE VENOMS

Getting bitten by a poisonous spider, scorpion, or snake in the wild could end your life, but encountering their venom at a hospital might actually save it! Animal venoms are complex brews of enzymes, toxins, and other chemicals that scientists can manipulate to make medicines. Already, chemists have mined venoms to concoct drugs that lower high blood pressure, target cancer cells, relieve arthritis, and treat muscular dystrophy. Death-stalker scorpions have never felt so used!

ROBO-ROACH

The little electronic backpacks glued to the cockroaches at Tokyo University do little to improve the ugly bugs' appearance, but they certainly enhance the roaches' function. No longer scurrying for food and spreading feces under the fridge, these hot-wired cockroaches now do the bidding of scientists who steer them like little, radio control cars. These robo-roach wranglers hope to fit the bugs with tiny cameras and someday "drive" them into rubble to seek out earthquake victims.

WORLD TOILET **DAY**

Kiss your commode every November 19, when the World Toilet Organization calls attention to the **2.6 BILLION** people across the globe who lack access to such a crucial convenience.

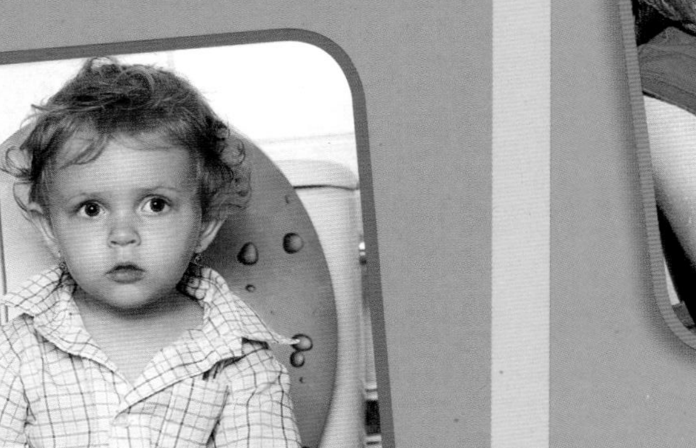

SNEEZE **DAY**

February 2 marks the anniversary of the **FIRST MOVIE RECORDING** of a sneeze, filmed way back in 1894. Sounds like it's due for a 3D sequel!

NATIONAL HAIRBALL AWARENESS **DAY**

Every April, celebrate the **GROSSEST NATURAL PRODUCT** of America's cat population with this holiday that promotes kitty grooming.

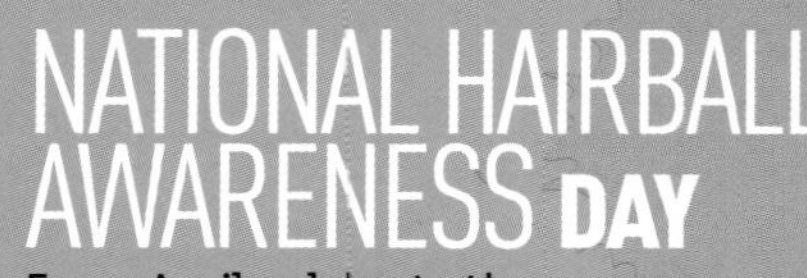

Disgusting DAYS

GAG GAUGE

HOME INVADERS

Daryl the Dung Beetle Ranks UNWELCOME GUESTS

CHAPTER 8

Disgusting Fun!

WE ALL KNOW "SOMEONE" with a horrible hobby (scab collecting, perhaps, or mastering the fine art of burp-talking). Hey, we're not about to point fingers or poop on anyone's party. Instead, we've come up with foul and fun activities—from gross games to wretched recipes—that are suitable for polite society. If you still feel the urge to belch the alphabet after finishing this chapter, however, knock yourself out!

YOU'RE NOT JUST TALKING TO YOUR PALS WHEN YOU GAB ON YOUR CELL PHONE. That shiny piece of glass and plastic is crawling with millions of bacteria—nearly 20 times the amount of germs you'll find on a typical toilet's flush handle. Now that's some gross gabbing!

It's only natural that your phone is awash with bacteria. You text with filthy fingers, dribble spittle when you talk, and clutch the gizmo against your greasy face. If you're going to share your conversations with an entire microscopic community, you might as well get to know the little eavesdroppers. Here's what you need to call a meeting with the microbes—with your parents' permission, of course.

It Came From Your SMART PHONE!

EQUIPMENT

- **Petri dishes prepared with agar**
  (see description in step 1)
- **Sterile cotton swabs**
- **Masking tape**
- **A cell phone**
  (or any other source of bacteria, such as your hand, a dish sponge, your dog's tongue, etc.)
- **Bleach**

DIRECTIONS

Step 1

Although growing bacteria is as easy as leaving an egg-salad sandwich in the attic, you'll need some specialized gear to collect and cultivate the little clingers from your phone. Online you'll find many stores that sell Petri dishes prepared with agar, a sweet gel that bacteria love to live on. You'll also need to buy some sterile swabs (which often come with the dishes).

Step 2

Once you have your Petri dish prepped with agar and warmed to room temperature, it's time to collect your sample. Remove a swab from its sterile packaging and wipe it across the face of your phone, taking care not to swipe anything else.

Step 3

Now rub the swab gently across the agar substance in the Petri dish. Replace the dish's cover and tape it shut. If you decide to take multiple samples from different surfaces—your keyboard, your toilet, your mouth—be sure to use a fresh swab and a new Petri dish for each new source of bacteria. Label the dishes so you know what's what.

Step 4

Store your dish in a hot spot—the toastier the better—for 36 to 48 hours. Keep it out of sunlight, if possible. Never open the dish once you've begun the growing process—no matter how tasty it might look! Bacteria associated with poop and food poisoning have been found on phones.

Step 5

A watched Petri dish never grows, so resist the urge to seek signs of life for at least 36 hours. By day two, you'll spy nasty clusters of little microbes. Just think: These germs are crawling on your phone when you hold it to your face! Take them on a tour of the house. Show them to your friends at school. Perhaps the microbes would like to meet the people they've heard so much about.

Step 6

Once you're done spending quality time with your little phone friends, ask a parent to open the Petri dish's lid and pour a bit of bleach into the agar. That'll kill your culture for proper disposal, but don't despair—there's more bacteria where that came from!

DARYL THE DUNG BEETLE'S FOUL FACTS

BE HAPPY you don't have any *Thiomargarita namibiensis* bacteria crawling on your phone. The **WORLD'S LARGEST BACTERIUM,** each one is the size of the period at the end of this sentence.

SEA PIG

IT'S TIME TO PUT YOUR NEWFOUND KNOWLEDGE OF CREEPY CREATURES TO THE TEST. Some of the following extreme animals are real. Can you spot the bona fide wildlife from the fearsome phonies? (Answers at the bottom of page 159.)

REAL, OR JUST REALLY UGLY?

PINK FAIRY ARMADILLO

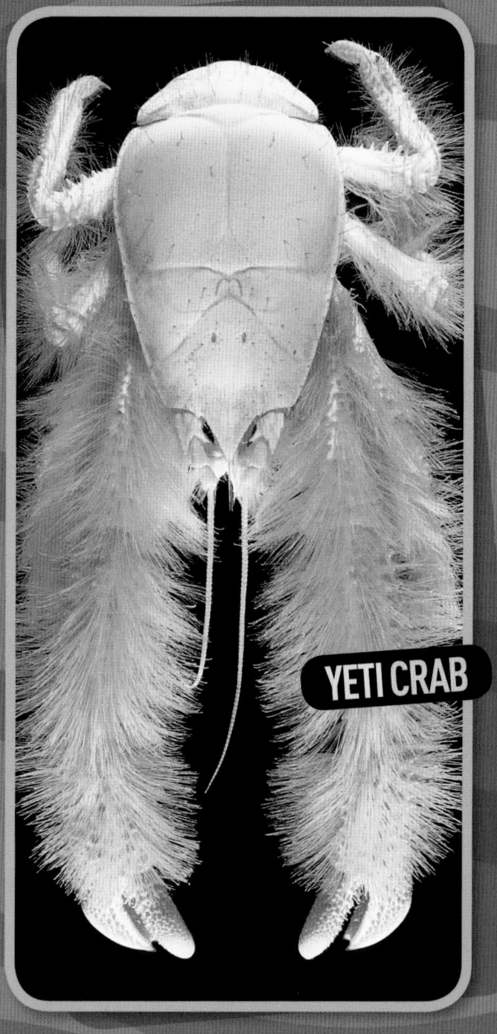

Answers: Trick question! They are all real.

Supplement your natural snot supply with this slimy formula . . .

Make YOUR OWN Mucus!

Ingredients

Clear school glue, such as Elmer's

Water

Borax laundry booster

(ask your parents to get some from the store's detergent aisle)

Food coloring

(green or yellow)

Directions

Step 1

Stir a spoonful of Borax into a cup of hot water. Mix it until the Borax is mostly dissolved.

Step 2

Squeeze ½ cup (118 ml) of glue into a bowl. Stir in ½ cup (118 ml) of water.

Step 3

Add a few drops of food coloring to the glue-and-water mix. Green mucus is often a sign of sickness, so decide if you want healthier-looking yellow snot... or not.

Step 4

Empty your Borax solution into the glue bowl and mix the whole mess with your hands. Presto! The slime will begin to form before your eyes! Add a tad more Borax if the snot's too runny.

Step 5

Pluck the artificial mucus from the bowl and take pride in your creation. Bottle it! Take it to the movies! Hang it from your nostrils—preferably in front of your sister! Make sure to store it in a baggie so it won't become boogerfied.

UP CLOSE & *Gross*

CAN YOU IDENTIFY THESE SIX ANIMALS OR OBJECTS— all of which were featured earlier in the book—from their extremely gross close-ups?

(Answers at the bottom of page 163.)

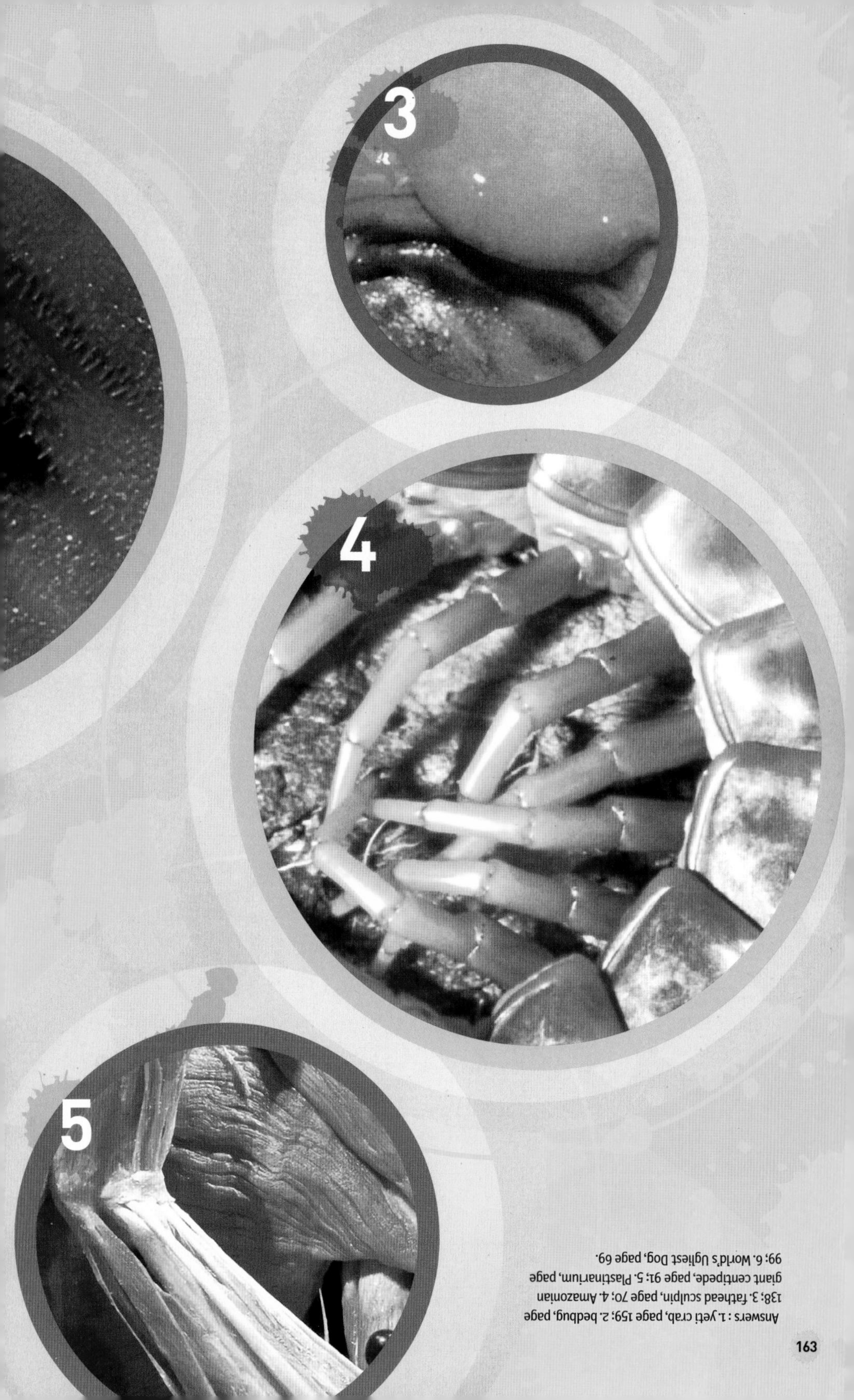

Answers : 1. yeti crab, page 159; 2. bedbug, page 138; 3. fathead sculpin, page 70; 4. Amazonian giant centipede, page 91; 5. Plastinarium, page 99; 6. World's Ugliest Dog, page 69.

Worm-Charm SCHOOL

BIRDS DO IT. FISHERMEN MASTERED THE TECHNIQUE CENTURIES AGO. And if you recall the sickening pastimes from chapter 6, it's even a spectator sport. Welcome to the world of worm charming, also known as "worm grunting" or "worm fiddling." Whatever the name, the method is the same: Charmers enchant earthworms with vibrations that penetrate deep into the ground. The worms—afraid that the sound is coming from a hungry mole digging in their direction—freak out and escape to the surface, only to be caught for bait or bragging rights.

Worm charming isn't just a people pastime; wood turtles and certain seagulls have learned the trick, too. Scientists call it "exploitive mimicry" because it copies a sound that earthworms fear and fools them into exposing themselves for capture. It's a behavior that will work to your benefit if you ever crave some slimy company. All you need is some patience and the right gear to master the art of worm charming.

DARYL THE DUNG BEETLE'S FOUL FACTS

THE RECORD NUMBER of worms caught in 30 minutes at the annual World Worm-Charming Championships is **567.** Can you top that?

EQUIPMENT

- A bucket (for collecting worms)
- One sturdy stick (2 feet/60 cm long by at least 2 inches/5 cm wide)
- A file tool (ask to borrow one from your parents)

DIRECTIONS

STEP 1

Find a flat patch of damp ground, preferably first thing in the morning. Remember, the early bird charms the worm.

STEP 2

If you have a stick and a file, first drive the stick vertically about halfway into the ground. Take the file and rub it repeatedly across the top of the stick in a rhythmic motion.

STEP 3

Sooner or later, your vibrations will "charm" the earthworms to the surface. See how many you can catch in a 30-minute period. Maybe bring a few home to show how charming you've become!

CREATIVE CHARMING

Half the fun of worm charming—actually, make that all the fun—is coming up with wacky ways to lure slimy squigglers to the surface. Take a cue from competitors in the World Worm-Charming Championships and break out stereo speakers or some rhythm instruments. (Worms *love* xylophones and drums.) Invent your own vibration-creating contraptions. The worst that can happen is you'll spend the morning in the dirt looking incredibly silly.

It won't roll over or play fetch, but a **HISSING COCKROACH** might make someone retch!

RAISE A Repulsive PET!

One of the largest members of the cockroach family, this thumb-size insect is quite harmless—and even friendly to its owners. It's also a movie star! When you see a fat, slimy cockroach in a film, chances are it's a hissing cockroach. Good luck training your new pet to sign autographs!

WHERE YOU GET ONE

Unless you're willing to go "hisser" hunting on the island of Madagascar, homeland of these fat-bodied bugs, your roach-collection options are limited to the World Wide Web. Many exotic pet-peddling sites (such as www.kenthebugguy.com) sell them.

HOW YOU RAISE IT

Buy a large rubber storage container or a glass tank (10 gallons/38 liters or larger) and fill the bottom with a thin layer of shredded newspaper or shredded wheat bran (known as "bran substrate" in exotic-pet circles). Smear the inside with a thin strip of petroleum jelly so the hisser can't climb out (they can't fly like other roaches), and secure the top with a mesh screen just to be safe. Last thing you want is a wayward hisser waking up Mom!

Drop in a wet sponge for water, and feed your roach fruits, veggies, and dog food. Hissers are social roaches, so they are fun to watch in small groups. Competing males will butt heads. Couples will mate and lay eggs if you keep their tank above 85°F (29°C), so adjust the temperature accordingly if you're not keen on cockroach babies!

BEST TRICK

True to their name, these roaches will hiss loudly when disturbed or competing for mates. Sometimes, they'll hiss in chorus for mysterious reasons.

HOW BADLY DO YOU want a season pass to a theme park? Six Flags Great America in Illinois will gladly give you one if you eat the most **HISSING** cockroaches in its annual Halloween eating contest!

If you're going to dabble in entomophagy—the eating of bugs—you might as well start with dessert. Ask your parents for help baking this tasty recipe from Zack Lemann, **"executive bug chef"** at New Orleans' Audubon Insectarium.

BAKE CHOCOLATE-CHiRP COOKiES!

iNGREDiENTS

- 2 ¼ cups (510 g) all-purpose flour
- 1 teaspoon baking soda
- 1 teaspoon salt
- 2 sticks butter, softened
- ¾ cup (170 g) granulated sugar
- ¾ cup (170 g) packed brown sugar
- 1 teaspoon vanilla extract
- 2 large eggs
- 2 cups (450 g) semi-sweet chocolate chips (one 12 oz. package)
- ½ cup (113 g) chopped dry-roasted crickets
- ½ cup (113 g) whole dry-roasted crickets

Where can I buy my edible bugs?

www.edible.com
http://importfood.com/thai_insects.html
http://thailandunique.com/

WARNING!
Don't eat any insects if you're allergic to shellfish.

DiRECTiONS

STEP 1

Preheat oven to 375°F (190°C).

STEP 2

Combine flour, baking soda, and salt in small bowl.

STEP 3

Beat butter, granulated sugar, brown sugar, and vanilla extract in large mixing bowl until it's good and creamy.

STEP 4

Add eggs to the larger mixing bowl, one at a time, beating well after each addition.

STEP 5

Gradually beat in the flour mixture. Stir in chocolate chips and chopped crickets.

STEP 6

Drop rounded tablespoons of your cricket cookie mix onto ungreased baking sheets. Top each cookie with three whole crickets.

STEP 7

Bake for nine to 11 minutes or until golden brown. Cool on baking sheets for two minutes, then remove to wire racks to finish cooling.

STEP 8

Take a bite. Congratulations—you're officially an entomophagist!

THERE'S MORE THAN ONE WAY to cook a cricket! If you'd rather try them baked without the cookie, arrange the insects on a **ROASTING PAN** and cook them in the oven at 375°F (190°C) for 30 minutes.

Everything you need to grow some bold mold!

SLIME TIME

If you already have a dog, why not raise a friendly puddle of dog vomit? That's exactly what a slime mold looks like: a greasy blob of gooey mucus. Neither plant nor animal, a slime mold is a fungus-like life-form that creeps across the forest floor on the hunt for bacteria.

WHERE YOU GET ONE

Slime molds flourish in damp forests under rotten logs. You might also find them oozing across your yard after a steady rain, which often triggers a growth spurt in these little bags of protoplasm. When residents of Dallas, Texas, encountered a slime-mold outbreak in 1973, they feared it was an alien invasion!

HOW YOU RAISE IT

Line a jar with a moist paper towel and drop in a chunk of slime mold (cutting them apart doesn't hurt them). Feed it a flake or two of raw oatmeal. Loosely screw on the lid and place the jar in a dark place. Each day, sprinkle your slime mold with water and drop in a few more oatmeal flakes. Make sure to keep an eye on your slime. These natural escape artists can climb out of most enclosures (although they do it very slowly).

BEST TRICK

Slime molds can figure out the shortest route through a maze to find food. Can your dog do that trick?

Host Your Own GROSS GRUDGE MATCH!

IT'S TIME TO CROWN THE REAL KING OF STINK, THE MASTER OF NASTINESS, THE TONY HAWK OF TOE JAM! We've organized four foul events that will decide who's the most gross among your friends and family. All you'll need is a judge with an iron stomach (a parent or sibling will do) and some competitors willing to play dirty for this dubious honor. Let the gross games begin!

EVENT 1: BAD-BREATH BATTLE

To capture the fragrance of that foul fog in your mouth, grab a spoon by the handle and slide it along the top of your tongue, starting at the back. Wait a minute for the saliva to dry on your spoon, then hand it to the judge for a sniff test. Now would also be a good time to thank your judge for displaying such bravery and devotion. Whoever's spoon is deemed most stinky wins this event.

SCORE-BOOSTING TIPS: Skipping your morning tooth-brushing routine will ensure your mouth is maxed out with odor-producing bacteria and putrid food particles.

EVENT 2: BOLDEST B.O.

This next round really stinks! Each contestant gets five minutes to run around the backyard, do some jumping jacks, drop to the floor for push-ups, and try any other activity that works up a good sweat. Then, your unfortunate judge takes a whiff of each contestant's armpits. Whoever has the stinkiest pits wins this round!

SCORE-BOOSTING TIPS: Glands in your armpits release an especially smelly set of chemicals, but you can boost their stink potential by letting bacteria collect in your sweat zones. In other words, don't bathe on the morning before your gross games!

FINAL EVENT: DANDRUFF DUMP

Being flaky is a good thing for this event! Each contestant will need a black piece of construction paper or dark cloth that will serve as his or her dandruff catcher. Contestants get 30 seconds to shake dead skin from their scalps onto their respective catchers. The judge will examine each catcher to see whose head spawned the biggest skin blizzard.

SCORE-BOOSTING TIPS: Not washing your hair will make for more flakes. Also, scratching your scalp with your fingernails while shaking your head dislodges more dandruff.

IN THE EVENT OF A TIE: TURN TO THE TOE JAM!

IF TWO OR MORE PLAYERS END THE COMPETITION WITH THE SAME SCORE, IT'S TIME FOR THE FOUL FINALE! Tied competitors must immediately whip off their socks and display their tootsies to the judge. Whoever has the most toe jam wins! You always knew that cheesy gunk between your toes would come in handy!

HOW TO SCORE: The maximum score for each event is set by the number of participants. The more people playing, the higher the maximum score. For example, if you have four players, the first-place finisher gets four points, second place gets three, third place gets two, and last place gets one. At the end of all events, each contestant adds up his or her points. Whoever has the most points is the most gross. If the winner happens to be you, congratulations! Now, do the world a favor and go brush your teeth.

RUNNY NOSE **SOAP DISPENSER**

Stick this schnoz to your shower wall and scrub-a-dub-dub with snotty soap.

PEE **PUCK**

A prank for your toilet tank, this tablet turns commode water yellow so it looks unflushed for days!

MEATBALL **BUBBLE GUMBALLS**

Blow meaty bubbles with this chewy treat. (Don't worry—it doesn't actually taste like meat!)

Real GAG GIFTS

CREDITS

Dedicated to Brevibacterium linens, the itty-bitty bacteria that raises a big stink on your feet. —CB

ILLUSTRATION CREDITS

AY: Alamy, CB: Corbis, DT: Dreamstime.com, GI: Getty Images, PR: Photo Researchers, NGS: National Geographic Stock, NC: Newscom, SS: Shutterstock

Cover: (tarsier), Alain Compost/Biosphoto; (skunk), Tom Brakefield/GI; (cockroach), Redmond Durrell/AY; (sneeze), Peter Cade/GI; (bird), Genevieve Vallee/AY; (rat), Andalucia Plus Image bank/AY; (woman), Chip Simons/GI; (bird waste), Dmitrijs Bindemanis/SS; Back Cover: (Darryl the dung beetle illustration), Clayton Hanmer; (cockroaches), Redmond Durrell/Alamy 1, Gary Dublanko/AY; 1-9 cockroaches, Redmond Durrell/AY; 2-3, Nicholas Eveleigh/AY; 2 (Right), V&A Images/AY; 3 (Left), Jim Snyders/AY; 3 (Right), Paul Hilton/EPA/NC; 4 (Top), Tier Und Naturfotografie/J & C Sohns/GI; 4 (Bottom), Jim and Jamie Dutcher/NGS; 5 (Top), Ralph Lee Hopkins/NGS; 5 (Bottom), Gregory G. Dimijian, M.D./PR, Inc.; 6 (Top Left), Steve Gschmeissner/PR, Inc.; 6 (Top, Right), Image Source/AY; 6 (Bottom, Left), WoodyStock/AY; 6 (Bottom, Right), Medical-on-Line/AY; 7 (Top, Left), Ted Kinsman/PR, Inc.; 7 (Top, Right), Jim Grace/PR, Inc.; 7, (Darryl the dung beetle illustration), Clayton Hanmer; 8, Margarita Borodina/ SS; 9 (Darryl the dung beetle illustration), Clayton Hanmer; 9 (Right), Redmond Durrell/AY 10-11 (Background), Goodshoot/Jupiter Images; 10-11 (Top), Andrzej Tokarski/AY; 10 (Top, Left), Cultura/Jupiter Images; 10 (Top, Center), Punchstock; 10 (Bottom, Left), Jupiter Images 10 (Bottom, Center Left), Royalty-Free/CB; 10 (Bottom, Center Right), Hannamariah/DT; 10 (Bottom, Right), Max Power/CB; 11 (Top), Jupiter Images; 11 (Bottom), Farek/DT; Chapter 1: 13, Eric Anthony Johnson/GI; 14, Gkanivets/DT; 15 (Background), SuperStock/GI; 15 (Bottom), Sumnersgraphicsinc/DT; 16-17 (Background, Center), Igorkovalchuk/DT; 16-17 (Center), Milos Luzanin/SS; 16-17 (Left, Top, and Right), Dr. Flash/SS; 16 (Top), Paulcowan/DT; 17 (Top), Griffin024/ DT; 17 (Bottom), Crisp/DT; 18-19 (Background), Nicholas Eveleigh/AY; 18 (Right), V&A Images/AY; 19 (Left), Jim Snyders/AY; 19 (Right), EPA/NC; 20, Drzaribu/DT; 21 (Top), Dreamframer/AY; 21 (Center), Mary Evans Picture Library/PR, Inc.; 21 (Bottom), Cammeraydave/DT; 22, Robert Clark/NGS; 23 (Top), Ulla Lohmann/NGS; 23 (Center), Kenneth Garrett/NGS;23 (Bottom), Enrico Ferorelli/NGS; 24-25 (Background), mountainpix/SS; 24, digitalSTOCK; 25 (Top), SPL/PR, Inc.; 25 (Bottom), Ralukatudor/DT; 26-27 (Background), Freeteo/DT; 26 (Bottom), ARENA Creative/SS; 27 (Top, Left), Slapster/AY; 27 (Top, Right), PR/AY; 27 (Bottom, Left), INTERFOTO/AY; 27 (Bottom, Right), Prisma Bildagentur AG/AY; 28, Selena/ SS; 29, INTERFOTO/AY; 30 (Top), NASA; 30 (Bottom), Robert Clark/NGS; 30-31 (Background), Robert Clark/NGS; 31 (Top, Left), ANSA/ANSA/CB; 31 (Top, Right), Public Domain; 31 (Bottom), Photo courtesy of Rick Gibson; 32 (Top, Left), North Wind Picture Archives/AY; 32 (Top, Right), Mary Evans Picture Library 2010; 32 (Center), North Wind Picture Archives/AY; 32 (Bottom, Left), Sianc/DT; 32 (Bottom, Right), DIZ Muenchen GmbH, Sueddeutsche Zeitung Photo/AY; Chapter 2: 35, photobank.ch/SS; 36-37 (Background), zentilia/SS; 37 (Top, Left), Sebastian Kaulitzki/SS; 37 (Top, Right), PR RM/GI; 37 (Bottom, Left), Science Photo Library/AY; 37 (Bottom, Right), PR RM/GI; 38-39, Aurora Creative/ GI; 40, B. Slaven MD/Custom Medical Stock ; 41 (Top), Sebastian Kaulitzki/SS; 41 (Center), Artvet/DT; 41 (Bottom), Mark Grenier/SS; 42-43 (Background), Jim Allan/ AY; 42, Lee Reitz/SS; 43 (Top, Left), Mikael Damkier/SS; 43 (Top, Right), CLIPAREA/Custom media/SS; 43 (Bottom, Left), CLIPAREA/Custom media/SS; 43 (Bottom, Right), Firma V/SS; 44 (Top, Left), Steve Gschmeissner/PR, Inc.; 44 (Top, Right), Image Source/AY; 44 (Bottom, Left), WoodyStock/AY; 44 (Bottom, Right), Medical-on-Line/AY; 45 (Top, Left), Ted Kinsman/PR, Inc.; 45 (Top, Right), Jim Grace/PR, Inc.; 45 (Bottom), Science Photo Library/AY; 46-47 (Background), Science Faction/ GI; 46 (Top, Left), UpperCut Images/AY; 46 (Top, Right), Scott Camazine/AY; 46 (Bottom, Left), Martin Muránsky/SS; 46 (Bottom Center), Brian Maudsley/SS; 46 (Bottom, Right), Michael Rosskothen/SS; 48, CREATISTA/SS; 49, Digital Vision; 50- 51, Jon Bower London/AY; 52-53, Rob Walls/AY; 54 (Top, Left), Flickr RF/GI; 54 (Top, Right), H. Mark Weidman Photography/AY; 54 (Bottom), JPagetRFphotos/SS; Chapter: 3; 57, Elena Butinova/SS; 58-59, DantÈ Fenolio/PR, Inc.; 59 (Left), blickwinkel/AY; 60, Elnur/SS; 61 (Top, Left), Michael and Patricia Fogden/NGS; 61 (Top, Right), Otto Plantema/FN/Minden Pictures/NGS; 61 (Right, Center), Mauricio Handler/NGS; 61 (Bottom, Left), Ben Horton/NGS; 61 (Bottom, Right), Chris Johns/NGS; 62 (Top), ocram/SS; 62 (Bottom, Left), Kathy Wright/ AY; 62 (Bottom, Right), Jane Burton/naturepl.com; 63 (Top), StudioSource/AY; 63 (Bottom), Eric Isselée/SS; 64 (Top), SS; 64 (Bottom, Left), imagebroker/AY; 64 (Bottom, Right), Rodger Tamblyn/AY; 65 (Top), Julian Clune/AY; 65 (Bottom), deepspacedave/SS; 66 (Top), Juergen & Christine Sohns/GI; 66 (Bottom), Jim and Jamie Dutcher/NGS; 67 (Top), Ralph Lee Hopkins/NGS; 67 (Bottom), Gregory G. Dimijian, M.D./PR, Inc.; 68 (Top, Left), Pisces Sportfishing Fleet/Rex USA; 68 (Top, Right), ChinaFotoPress/GI; 68 (Bottom), Ho New/Reuters; 69 (Left), NC; 69 (Right), Westley Hargrave/Splash News/NC; 70 (Top), © NORFANZ 2003 Founding Parties; 70-71 (Background), Willyam Bradberry/SS; 70 (Bottom, Left), Yusuke Yoshino/Nature Production/Minden Pictures; 70 (Bottom, Right), Doc White/naturepl.com; 71 (Top), Doug Allan/naturepl.com; 71 (Bottom), AFP/GI/NC; 72, Joel Sartore/NGS; 73, SuperStock; 74 (Top), © Martin Withers/FLPA/Minden Pictures; 74 (Bottom), Birgitte Wilms/MindenPictures/NGS; 75 (Top), Thomas Marent/Minden Pictures/NGS; 75 (Center), Paul Sutherland/NGS; 75 (Bottom), Kim Taylor/naturepl.com; 76 (Top, Left), Vetta/GI; 76 (Top, Right), imagebroker/AY; 76 (Bottom), Purestock/GI; Chapter 4: 79, Zoediak/DT; 80 (Top), Cosmin Manci/SS; 80 (Center), Kasza/SS; 80 (Bottom), Pan Xunbin/SS; 81 (Top, Left), Inventori/DT; 81 (Top, Right), Buckskinman/DT; 81 (Bottom, Left), Zralok/DT; 81 (Bottom, Right), Dja65/SS; 82-83 (Background), Orionmystery/DT; 82 (Bottom), Rolf Nussbaumer/naturepl.com; 83 (Top, Left), Hudakore/DT; 83 (Top, Right), Mazdak Radjainia; 83 (Bottom), Rod Williams/ naturepl.com; 84-85 (Background), Eky Studio/SS; 84 (Top), Jolanta Dabrowska/AY; 84 (Top Center), cbimages/AY; 84 (Center), Nature Picture Library/ naturepl.com; 84 (Bottom Center), Stephen Dalton/PR, Inc.; 84 (Bottom), John T. Fowler/AY; 85 (Top), ostill/SS; 85 (Bottom), AJP/SS; 86 (Top), H Lansdown/AY; 86 (Center), Vaclav Volrab/SS; 86 (Bottom), Melinda Fawver/SS; 87, Cuiphoto/SS; 88-89, maska/SS; 88 (Left), Scott Camazine/AY; 89 (Top, Left), Science Photo Library/ AY; 89 (Top, Right), Darlyne A. Murawski/NGS; 89 (Bottom, Left), PR RM/GI; 89 (Bottom, Right), Amazon-Images/AY; 90-91 (Background), Will & Deni McIntyre/GI; 90 (Top), blickwinkel/AY; 91 (Top), Papilio/AY; 91 (Top Center), Dr. Morley Read/PR, Inc.; 91 (Bottom Center), blickwinkel/AY; 91 (Bottom), AFP/GI/NC; 92 (Top), Ivan Kuzmin/SS;92 (Bottom), Premaphotos/AY; 93 (Top), Koshevnyk/SS; 93 (Center), PR RM/GI; 93 (Bottom), Louise Murray/AY; 94 (Top, Left), papkin/SS; 94 (Top, Right), Ivan Kmit/AY; 94 (Bottom), Ryan M. Bolton/SS; Chapter 5: 97, Dinoforlena/DT; 98 (Top), Richard Malpas/AY; 98 (Bottom), Anne Lewis/AY; 99 (Top), Zahler/DT; 99 (Left), ClassicStock/AY; 99 (Right), Caro/AY; 100, Eric Brown/ AY; 101 (Top), Boaz Rottem/AY; 101 (Bottom, Left), FLPA/AY; 101 (Bottom, Right), Ben Lewis/AY; 102-103, Philip Dalton/naturepl.com; 104-105 (Background), EPA/ CB/NGS; 104 (Bottom), Toni Vilches/AY; 105 (Top), Image Source/GI; 105 (Center), DAJ/GI; 105 (Bottom), AP Images/Tina Fineberg; 106-107 (Background), Scripps Institution of Oceanography, UC San Diego; 106 (Top), Peter Bennett/NC; 107 (Left), Peter Bennett/Ambient Images/NC; 107 (Right), J. Leichter, Scripps Institution of Oceanography, UC San Diego; 108 (Top), Foodcollection/GI; 108 (Left Center), Bon Appetit/AY; 108 (Right Center), Szefei/DT; 108 (Bottom), Nordicphotos/AY; 109 (Left), Richgerrish/DT; 109 (Right), Neil Setchfield/AY; 110 (Top), Danita Delimont/AY; 110 (Bottom), Anders Ryman/AY; 111 (Top), Mar Photographics/ AY; 111 (Center), DK. Khattiya/AY; 111 (Bottom), Mar Photographics/AY; 112-113, Fiona Fanning/National Geographic My Shot; 114 (Top), WILDLIFE GmbH/AY; 114 (Bottom), Brian Yarvin/AY; 115 (Top), AP Images/Howie Rumberg; 115 (Center), Franco Pizzochero/AY; 115 (Bottom), Rebecca Hale, NGP; 116 (Top, Left), Ia64/DT; 116 (Top, Right), Amorphis/DT; 116 (Center), Czuber/DT; 116 (Bottom, Left), neil setchfield yuckfood.com/AY; 116 (Bottom, Right), D. Hurst/AY; Chapter 6: 119 (Left), 20th Century Fox/Paramount/The Kobal Collection/Art Resource, NY; 119 (Center), Dreamworks LLC/The Kobal Collectoin/Art Resource, NY; 119 (Right), Lucas Films/20th Century Fox/The Kobal Collection/Art Resource, NY; 120 (Top), ZUMA Press/NC; 120 (Center), Lucas Films/20th Century Fox/The Kobal Collection/Art Resource, NY; 120 (Bottom), Dreamworks LLC/The Kobal Collection/Art Resource, NY; 121 (Top), ITAR-TASS/NC; 121 (Center), WoodyStock/ AY; 121 (Bottom), Globe Photos/Zuma Press; 122 (Top), Paramount/The Kobal Collection/Art Resource, NY; 122 (Bottom), Cartoon Network/Warner Bros./The Kobal Collection/Art Resource, NY; 123 (Top), Warner Bros./The Kobal Collection/Art Resource, NY; 123 (Bottom), © 2007 by Entertainment Pictures/Zuma Press; 124-125 (Background), EPA/NC; 124 (Left), © Studio Wim Delvoye; 124 (Right), © Studio Wim Delvoye; 125 (Top), © Studio Wim Delvoye; 125 (Bottom), EPA/ Tamas Kovacs/NC; 126 (Top), AP Images/PA Wire/Press Association Images 2010; 126 (Bottom), Rogan Macdonald/eyevine/NC; 127 (Top), AP Images/Manuel Balce Ceneta; 127 (Center), Jeff Greenberg/AY; 127 (Bottom), Globe Photos/Zuma Press/NC; 128, Photos 12/AY; 129 (Top, Left), Image Ten/The Kobal Collection/ Art Resource, NY; 129 (Top Center), Vasilchenko Nikita/SS; 129 (Top, Right), AP Images/Felipe Dana; 129 (Bottom), City of Fruita; 130 (Top), UPPA/Photoshot/NC; 130 (Bottom, Left), AP Images/Sakchai Lalit; 130 (Bottom, Right), Rusgri/DT; 131 (Top), Jeffrey R. Werner/www.incrediblefeatures.com; 131 (Center), FilmMagic, Inc/GI; 131 (Bottom), AP Images/Prakash Hatvalne; 132 (Top), WENN.com/NC; 132 (Bottom), James R Ford; 133 (Top), Jordan Eagles, TSC20X20.4, 2011 (detail), Blood, copper preserved on plexiglass, UV resin; 133 (Center), Terence Bogue; 133 (Bottom), Adrienne Antonson; 134 (Top, Left), AP Images/Eric Gay; 134 (Top, Right), pzechner/AY; 134 (Bottom), Dale O'Dell/AY;Chapter 7: 137, Briancweed/DT; 138-139 (Top), MorganOliver/DT; 138-139 (Bottom), Deklofenak/SS; 140 (Top), Greg Wright/AY; 140 (Bottom), Okea/DT; 141 (Top), Timothy Camuso/AY; 141 (Bottom), National Geographic Image Collection/AY; 142 (Top), Johnfoto/DT; 142 (Left, Center), Deco/AY; 142 (Right, Center), Sebastian Kaulitzki/AY; 143 (Top), B-d-s/DT; 143 (Center), Persiki12/DT; 143 (Bottom), Picstudio/DT; 144 (Top), 3355m/DT; 144 (Bottom, Left), Ra3rn/DT; 144 (Bottom, Center), Gvictoria/DT; 144 (Bottom, Right), ammeraydave/DT; 144-145 (Background), Krasnaok/DT; 145 (Right), Gustavotoledo/DT; 146-147 (Background), LukaTDB/SS; 146 (Top), Dorling Kindersley RF/GI; 147 (Bottom), Robert Harding Picture Library Ltd/AY; 148-149 (Background), Jaboardm/DT; 148 (Bottom), Paulvinten/DT; 149 (Top, Left), Efired/DT; 149 (Top, Right), Lightworks Media/AY; 149 (Bottom, Left), Rebecca Hale, NGP; 149 (Bottom, Right), Caimacanul/DT; 150 (Top), Louise Murray/AY; 150 (Bottom), Rebecca Hale, NGP; 151 (Top), Volker Steger/PR, Inc.; 151 (Bottom), AP Images/Katsumi Kasahara; 152 (Top), Hshii/DT; 152 (Center), Mandy Goodbehear/SS; 152 (Bottom), Fiamoli/DT;Chapter 8: 155, Catherine Lall/SS; 156-157 (Bottom, Background), Rebecca Hale, NGP; 156 (Background, Bottom, Left), Michal Kowalski/SS; 156 (Bottom, Right), Awcnz62/DT; 157 (Top), Awcnz62/DT; 157 (Bottom), Michal Kowalski/SS; 158 (Top), AP Images Richard O'Driscoll; 158 (Bottom), PR RM/GI; 159 (Top, Left), Doug Perrine/naturepl.com; 159 (Right), Michel Segonzac/NGS; 159 (Bottom, Left), Michael Nichols/NGS; 160, Felix Mizioznikov/SS; 161 (Top), Plasticrobot/DT; 161 (Bottom, Left), Devonyu/DT; 161 (Bottom, Right), Scantynebula/DT; 162 (Top, Left), Michel Segonzac/NGS; 162 (Top, Right), MorganOliver/DT; 162 (Bottom), Westley Hargrave/Splash News/NC; 163 (Top), © NORFANZ 2003 Founding Parties; 163 (Center), Papilio/AY; 163 (Bottom), Caro/AY; 164-165, Jan Tyler/iStockphoto; 164 (Left), Zoediak/DT; 165 (Top), Zoediak/DT; 165 (Bottom), Eric1513/DT; 166-167 (Background), Tim Whitby/AY; 166, Jdgrant/DT; 168 (Left), Sanclemenesdigpro/DT; 168 (Right), MShieldsPhotos/AY; 169, Theo Fitzhugh/AY; 170-171 (Background), WILDLIFE GmbH/AY; 171 (Top, Center, Bottom), Naturepix/AY; 172, Evan Sharboneau/DT; 173 (Top), Creatista/DT; 173 (Bottom), Hacstock78/DT; 174 (Top), © Archie McPhee; 174 (Center), courtesy of Locomolife.com; 174 (Bottom), Courtesy of Chris Cossalter/PeePuck; 175, Redmond Durrell/AY.

For information about special discounts for bulk purchases, please contact National Geographic Books Special Sales: ngspecsales@ngs.org

For rights or permissions inquiries, please contact National Geographic Books Subsidiary Rights: ngbookrights@ngs.org

For more information, please call 1-800-NGS LINE (647-5463) or write to the following address:
National Geographic Society
1145 17th Street N.W.
Washington, D.C. 20036-4688 U.S.A.

Paperback ISBN: 978-1-4263-1066-9
Library ISBN: 978-1-4263-1127-7

Printed in China
12/TS/1